CRACK THE FAT-LOSS CODE

Outsmart Your Metabolism and Conquer the Diet Plateau

WENDY CHANT, MPT, SPN

New York Chicago San Francisco Lisbon London Madrid Mexico City
Milan New Delhi San Juan Seoul Singapore Sydney Toronto

Library of Congress Cataloging-in-Publication Data

Chant, Wendy.
    Crack the fat loss code : outsmart your metabolism and conquer the diet plateau /
Wendy Chant; foreword by Sergio M. Zamora.
       p.   cm.
    Includes bibliographical references and index.
    ISBN-13: 978-0-07-154691-1 (alk. paper)
    ISBN-10:   0-07-154691-X (alk. paper)
    1. Weight loss.   2. Reducing diets.   I. Title.

RM222.2.C4394   2008
613.2'5—dc22   2007034051

To my daughter, Valerie; may you continue to always dream big,
accomplish much, and live lots! Mommy loves you!

This book is also dedicated to you, the reader, and to every person in
pursuit of a better body, better health, and a better life.

Best wishes for a life that's ForeverFit!

8 9 10 11 12 13 14 15 16 17 18 19 20 21   FGR/FGR   0 9

ISBN 978-0-07-154691-1
MHID   0-07-154691-X

McGraw-Hill books are available at special quantity discounts to use as premiums and sales promotions or for use in corporate training programs. To contact a representative, please visit the Contact Us pages at www.mhprofessional.com.

All information written in this guide or presented orally is the property of ForeverFit Lifestyle Centers, Inc., and such information may not be reproduced in any form without written consent from ForeverFit Lifestyle Centers, Inc.

ForeverFit Lifestyle Centers, Inc., and its staff do not represent themselves as medical or nutrition professionals. ForeverFit Lifestyle Centers, Inc., its staff, and programs make no claim to recommend, diagnose, treat, or cure any disease or complication by any holder or purchaser of this material. It is under the strong advice of ForeverFit Lifestyle Centers, Inc., that any and all individuals seek advice from their health care professional before undertaking any exercise or nutrition plan.

ForeverFit is a registered identity of ForeverFit Lifestyle Centers, Inc. Nutrition Boot Camp is a trademark of ForeverFit Lifestyle Centers, Inc., and no entity may use or market Nutrition Boot Camp.

This book is printed on acid-free paper.

Contents

    Carb-Deplete Day (A) Food Log   238
    Baseline Day (B) Food Log   239
    Carb-Down Day (C) Food Log   240
    Carb-Up Day (D) Food Log   241

12 **ForeverFit Eating: More of Wendy's
    "Mmm Good" Recipes**   243
    Breakfast Favorites   244
    Anytime Egg Favorites   246
    Salad and Side Dish Favorites   251
    Chicken and Fish Favorites   259

    Appendix A: Body Fat Calculator   265
    Appendix B: Metric Conversion Chart   267
    References and Scientific Basis   269
    More About ForeverFit Programs and Services   275
    Index   277

Foreword

As a plastic surgeon, I am used to people looking for quick fixes. In a sense, America is a country *full* of people looking for quick fixes. That is why both cosmetic surgery and the diet-book industry are so profitable. But both industries are ripe for opportunistic practitioners looking to provide as many quick fixes as consumers seek—and only as effective as the patient undergoing the procedure.

Personal accountability is the key to having a successful cosmetic procedure like liposuction or a tummy tuck, just as it is important to succeeding on a diet, whether it's South Beach or Atkins, Fit for Life or the Best Life diet. The best nutritionists and plastic surgeons know that menus and procedures take our clients only so far; the rest is up to them. The more information, education, and motivation we can give them, in addition to the products and services we offer, the better their results will be.

Wendy Chant is a close friend I've known for over two years now. But it only took me two seconds to realize she was the real deal: a nutrition and exercise expert who not only talked the talk but also walked the walk.

I met Wendy through a mutual friend who wouldn't stop talking about becoming "forever fit." I had to admit I was skeptical at first, but my friend swore by Wendy, and I knew I couldn't continue down the path to weight gain, lack of exercise, and processed food I was on any longer.

Wendy was tough but fair. I was impressed by her physique and her expertise. She wasn't touting some "fake food" product or overpriced T-shirt. Immediately I sensed that she really cared about me—and my progress. She put me through my paces, but more than just a quick fix, she gave me the tools I needed to succeed on my own.

I was hooked. Over the years I'd tried many diets, most of which helped me wind up right where I was—forty pounds overweight and fearing yet another diet plateau I'd never be able to break through. But I lost the weight, slowly and surely, through Wendy's proven system.

And I'm not alone. Every patient I've sent to Wendy since has lost weight and kept it off. That's because Wendy's program is more than a diet; it's a lifestyle. It teaches you how to eat what works for you rather than tell you what you *must* eat and *when*. It's not just another diet that lets you gain the weight back, because it's not just another diet. In fact, it's not a diet at all.

The lessons Wendy taught me in our eight weeks together gave me the tools I needed to succeed on my own. Her program is more than just a way to lose fat and keep it off; it's a way to control and maintain your weight.

Personally, I was thrilled to find Wendy Chant. Professionally, I'm just as pleased. Now I have an alternative for my patients—another option to try instead of costly and complicated surgical procedures.

Many of the people who come into my office aren't ready for surgery just yet. Maybe they're too heavy to sustain the demands of a procedure, or they're not heavy enough. When I send them to Wendy, they can be prepared both mentally and physically to undergo a surgical procedure to address their weight issues and keep it off by a combination of our two strategies.

I often say that Wendy gets them healthy first so that I can come in and sculpt their bodies second. It works better when the procedure is second to the cure. Having the procedure without the boot camp is a little like taking the pill without asking what it is first; you might get results, but without true understanding, how can they possibly last?

I was eager to write Wendy's foreword because, as a plastic surgeon specializing in body contouring and surgical bypasses, I think I have a unique perspective on what Wendy's clients, and mine, go through. Frankly, patients who only have the bypass are not as healthy or safe as those who go through Wendy first. Take it from me: natural weight loss is better. Bypass patients have more complications and far worse recoveries than Wendy's clients.

Part of Wendy's success, and the reason I'm so willing to refer patients to her (which is not something I do for other practitioners), is that her courses are so very easy to understand. She brings science to a very common language, so it's easier to understand why to do things; they make sense.

Oh, and if you're wondering why I know so much about Wendy Chant, ForeverFit, and Nutrition Boot Camp, it's because I'm a veteran. That's right. I went through Nutrition Boot Camp—and it changed my life. I lost forty pounds, and the best part is, after two years, I'm still working my program and have managed to keep the weight off. I'm a living example of Wendy's subtitle: I conquered my diet plateau—forever.

Once you know how to crack the fat-loss code, you can, too.

And there's no better teacher than Wendy Chant.

—Sergio M. Zamora, M.D., FACS

Acknowledgments

I would like to thank the following people for their tireless efforts and priceless contributions to the making of this book:

Rusty Fischer, for all his hard work, incredible professionalism, and kind spirit that made this book the best it could be.

Wendy Sherman, my literary agent, who believed in this book and my message and helped so passionately to get it published.

Judith McCarthy, Sarah Pelz, and McGraw-Hill for their consideration and work in publishing this book.

Rachel Dexter, my dearest friend, who through her amazing transformation and enthusiasm in the program for countless years has inspired so many lives. I thank her for all the help she has given me to continue to spread my message.

Love to my brother, Tom, and nephew, Robbie. As always, a special thanks to Diane Breen for her continued guidance, wisdom, and friendship. Thanks, Debbie and Jim Guthrie, for always lending a hand.

Kind appreciation to Monica Wofford for her guidance in getting this book started.

Much gratitude to Adam Williams and Sattva Productions for all their continued technical and production work for ForeverFit.

Sincere thanks to Blanch Torres, Vickie McVay, Laura Brown, Robyn Barnes, Dr. Sergio M. Zamora, Sandy Pemble, Susan Renzulli, Nancy Maddox, Dr. James Kornegay, Dr. Alan

Newman, Claire Evans, Jenny Young, and Jane Scrima for all the continued referrals and belief in me and the ForeverFit message.

Love and appreciation goes out to my love Scott Tate; to friends and supporters Donielle Deitz; Anita Weber; Debbie Barnes; Karen Fant; Eunice and Mike Bass; Ruth Coleman; Fenton Froom; Linda Chamberlain; Sonja and Chris Smith; Vickie Tsirigotis; the Myers and Zarbo family; Pam Simmons; Kim Perry; Ralph and Sharon Spano; Jackie Roberts; Debbie Cummings; Jana Weiner; Karyn Angel; Diane Thomson; Cathy Marquez; Mark Jarrell; Cheryl Lilly; Denise Charlesworth; Theresa Carter; Karen, Donna, and Ann Concannon; Tina Rudez; Tim Gardner; Elaine Gigicos; Ina Williams; Melissa Grisson; Ann Holstein; Jack Machise; Elaine Lavato; Denny Martin; Mary Ellen Dowdy; Jeanne Cooley; Chris Newton; Susan Newton; Rosemary and Jeff George; Carole Crowley; Lana Auld; my crew in Altamonte Springs, Leesburg, and New Smyrna Beach; and all my veteran boot campers for their friendship and support.

Introduction

You Can Transform Your
Body, Mind, and Spirit

Wouldn't it be great to understand the secret behind diet success? Wouldn't it be amazing to lose fat efficiently? What if you could have built-in "Food Passes" that allow you to eat out, have a drink, and celebrate in style—not in starvation? What if you could solve the age-old mystery of how to lose the fat—and keep it off?

Now you can. *Crack the Fat-Loss Code* takes the mystery out of your body, a machine that fights every effort you make to lose fat. By understanding the science behind the fat-loss code, you can conquer your old eating habits and crack the fat-loss code.

Losing unwanted weight is a serious challenge for many of us, in part because of the confusing glut of information and misinformation we're constantly exposed to. We've all heard the hype about "miracle" fad diets and "quick weight loss" exercise programs. But successful weight loss and a healthy lifestyle are possible only when you learn how to combine the science of proper nutrition with an exercise program tailored to your specific needs.

That is precisely the philosophy behind *Crack the Fat-Loss Code*. This unique program is based on the science of how your body digests, stores, and uses the food you consume. The eating plan is not a diet that forbids certain foods, but rather a macro-patterning program that regulates how and when you take in protein, fat, and carbohydrates to burn fat. Best of all, it allows you to *eat all foods*—such as bread, pasta, wine, and many more of your favorites—based on your body's hormonal status.

Good health is a marathon, not a sprint. It lasts a lifetime, so why not find a program that lasts a lifetime? Other diets let you down once you've lost the weight. *Crack the Fat-Loss Code* provides not only an intensive eight-week process for losing the fat, but also a lifelong maintenance program that fits with your lifestyle. This is no rigid system based on denial; the food plans are generous, simple, and easy to tailor to your own needs. Built-in Food Passes make it easy—and healthy—to rotate out the days so that you can party with the best of them and not throw the entire plan out of whack.

Code Cracker

Good health is a marathon, not a sprint. It lasts a lifetime, so why not find a program that lasts a lifetime?

The information and lessons in *Crack the Fat-Loss Code* are from real life, put in practice by people, including me, who walk the talk. Television, bookstores, magazines, and every other media outlet are perpetually flooded with diet, health, and fitness information and material written by people who never once practiced, dieted, or lived what they want you to do. With so many gimmicks and falsehoods, and so much misinformation on the market today—and more coming every day—it's no wonder if you're confused.

I meet people like you every day—people who are frustrated and at a loss to equate the bold claims of the latest diet fad with their lackluster results. That's why I made sure that before I ever sat down to write one word of *Crack the Fat-Loss Code*, I was prepared, personally and professionally.

I am a certified Master Personal Trainer and Specialist in Performance Nutrition, with a bachelor of science degree in medical sciences and nutrition science. I began my career as a personal trainer with Bally Total Fitness and then quickly achieved a national ranking as one of the top ten in personal training. My commitment to helping others achieve their goals eventually inspired me to open my own training studio, ForeverFit®, in 1998.

My experience is not limited to the classroom or the gym. I have run competitive marathons and competed as a champion bodybuilder on the national level. Now retired, I have committed to teaching full-time and am a sought-after speaker in the nutrition and fitness field. My unique food plan is not a fad diet or a quick fix; it is a lifestyle plan with no forbidden foods and plenty of room to fit into your busy, hectic schedule.

So why another diet book? Why a boot camp specifically designed for nutrition? Consider America's poor health trends:

- A recent *USA Today* survey stated that over 80 percent of Americans want to lose weight.
- Medical costs related to obesity add up to more than $40 billion annually.
- Heart disease is the number one killer in America, responsible for over 40 percent of all deaths.
- Sixty million Americans have been diagnosed with some form of cardiovascular disease.
- High blood pressure climbs 1 percent annually.
- A million new cases of diabetes are diagnosed each year.
- One in three Americans will develop cancer; some 80 percent of cancers are related to diet.
- Life expectancy decreases by six months for every pound by which a person is overweight.

But you don't need me to tell you what you already know: staying healthy is a full-time job! And it is; I have dedicated my life not only to keeping myself fit, but also to improving the health and well-being of others. The truly successful ones are those who get rid of words like *diets*, *fads*, and *trends* and make eating well a part of living well.

> ### 🔒 Code Cracker
> *Crack the Fat-Loss Code* takes the mystery out of your body, a machine that fights every effort you make to lose fat.

Crack the Fat-Loss Code cuts through the confusion with these features:

• **Eight weeks to efficient fat loss:** You read that right—*eight weeks* to efficient fat loss. In just two short months, you can break your diet plateau, forever.

• **A lifestyle, not a diet:** Most diets make *you* revolve around *them*. *Crack the Fat-Loss Code* does it the right way; the meal plans revolve around you. By allowing you generous portion control and complete personalization, the meal plans make it easy to eat out, enjoy the holidays, and celebrate along with everyone else.

• **The keys to a better body, better health, and better life:** Health doesn't exist in a vacuum. True health comes from the alignment of your body, your health, and your life. In this book I don't just tackle one; I tackle all three.

• **No gimmicks, just the truth:** This is no fad diet; it's not a diet at all. You'll find no trendy foods or advice here. When you've got the truth on your side, you don't need gimmicks.

- **The secret to becoming forever fit:** As I said, this is a lifestyle, not a diet. You have to eat to survive, so why not eat to thrive? Learning the science behind fat loss is a life lesson; there is no expiration date on knowledge.

- **The power of Nutrition Boot Camp:** Most boot camps revolve around exercise, but if you don't know how to eat right, exercise becomes like a Band-Aid on the bigger problem at large. My plan is designed for nutrition first, exercise second.

- **No forbidden foods:** To be forever fit takes a lifetime of food choices. That is why *Crack the Fat-Loss Code* contains *no* forbidden foods. It's your life; eat what you want!

- **A program that really works:** When you learn the science behind the fat-loss code and break it forever, you approach nutrition and fitness with the logic of knowledge, not the emotion of the latest diet book or fitness fad. When you know the fat-loss code, you can crack it. When you crack the fat-loss code, it can't *not* work.

The lessons and information in this book not only will last a lifetime but also will improve the time you have in life and finally give you the understanding and the correct information so you can take back control of your health and future well-being. Quality of life is the key to healthy living, and that's because our bodies and minds are inextricably linked. When you eat better, you feel better; when you feel better, life is better. It's just that simple.

Code Cracker
When you eat better, you feel better; when you feel better, life is better.

Consider the story of one of my star pupils, Rachel Dexter. Rachel struggled with obesity all of her life. Although she was the heaviest of five children, Rachel took to athletics early. Then a debilitating knee injury in 1988 forced Rachel to essentially cease all athletic activity. She was out of work for a year and on crutches for over six months.

While she was sidelined with her knee injury, Rachel's weight slowly increased to well over three hundred pounds. Not only were the mental effects of her weight isolating and debilitating, but the physical effects were life-threatening. Rachel was unwittingly putting her own life in danger.

Rachel received a wake-up call on her thirty-seventh birthday, when both her parents were diagnosed with diabetes. The news prompted her to visit her own doctor for a long-overdue physical. The doctor's message was blunt: "Rachel, by the time you're forty, you'll be a diabetic." Rachel was put on four types of medication to help treat her weight issue, and she began to experiment with different fad diets on the market.

Still feeling miserable, moody, and no closer to losing weight, Rachel was coming to the end of her rope. Then one day a mutual friend introduced her to me and ForeverFit. Uplifted and motivated by her newfound understanding, Rachel committed herself to the ForeverFit plan.

The results happened quickly. At the end of the first year, she had lost an amazing 107 pounds. The more the weight fell off, the more motivated Rachel became. Not only was the plan improving her physical health, but it was improving her attitude as well.

Like many who have cracked the fat-loss code, Rachel can even eat out if she wants to, because there are no forbidden foods on the ForeverFit plan. Once she was no longer the heaviest sibling in the family, Rachel could even motivate her parents and her twin sister to start the program. Thanks to ForeverFit, Rachel has drastically improved her lifestyle. Since beginning the program, she has lost 160 pounds. That's a whole person!

Today Rachel is one of my most valued employees, a true dynamo in the health field, and an invaluable member of the ForeverFit team.

Congratulations on making the right choice in the journey for a better body, better health, and better life. Continue to follow your lessons and walk the talk, and you, too, will truly be ForeverFit.

 FAT-LOSS FACT
Quality of life is the key to healthy living, and that's because our bodies and minds are inextricably linked.

PART 1

Why Your Body Won't Lose Fat

Your Body

The Ultimate Survivor

Your body is a survivor. In many ways, it is the *ultimate* survivor. The human body has evolved over thousands of years and managed to flourish long before bottled water, protein bars, and frozen foods. Whether it was ingesting saber-toothed tiger steaks or woolly mammoth burgers, roots and berries or twigs and stems, this miraculous body managed to fuel the performance of generations of vital, busy, active human beings.

The human body today is no different from the human body that wrote on cave walls, invented the wheel, discovered fire, built the Roman Empire, performed in the first-ever Olympics, created the alphabet, or explored the world.

That's because your body does one thing extremely well: it survives.

> **Code Cracker**
> The body disregards our own wants and needs for the betterment of our survival.

In this ultimate quest for survival, the body disregards our own wants and needs for the betterment of our survival. Always remember that, as you begin any diet, your body is already in alert response mode, like a battleship preparing for war. The body does not want to diet. In fact, the very last thing your body wants to do is diet.

The body does not care if you have a little extra weight on your bones. In fact, it *wants* a little extra weight on your bones, because extra weight means extra fuel for it to draw from. The more fuel it has in reserve, the less your body has to worry about where its next burst of energy is going to come from.

When it comes to food, the body is like the mother who knows best and does what's best for us, whether we like it or not. The body is the ultimate survivor. It has survived all of your attempts to lose weight. It has survived every cold, infection, cut, scrape, or fad diet you've ever inflicted upon it. Even alcohol, drugs, and our own appetite for self-destruction can't deny this ultimate survivor what it wants to do most: survive.

To beat the body at its own game and understand why it does what it does when it does it, keep reading!

FAT-LOSS FACT

The body does not want to diet. In fact, the very last thing your body wants to do is diet.

Understanding the Body's Needs

If you were to strip your life down to the bare-bottom basics, if you were to give up all your luxuries, books, CDs, aromatherapy candles, throw pillows, vacations, diamonds, and pearls, you as a human being would really need only three things to survive: food, shelter, and clothing.

Well, your body needs only three things to survive, too. Your body needs B.E.D. In other words, it needs to *breathe*, *eat*, and *drink*. Since I'm assuming you already know how to breathe and the good folks over at Evian have pretty much taught you everything you need to know about drinking eight glasses of water a day, I'm going to focus on the eating part.

Ready? It's real simple: Your body needs food to survive. In fact, your body always thinks the last thing you ate is the last thing you'll ever eat.

> ### Code Cracker
> To function, your body does a thousand things a day without you even thinking about it.

The next thing to remember is that the human body is a machine based on survival. It doesn't eat because food tastes good, looks good, is cooked by a world-renowned chef, or is served at a five-star restaurant. Your body eats for the same reason it does everything else: to survive.

To function, your body does a thousand things a day without you even thinking about it. When was the last time you had to be conscious of the need to take a breath, flex a muscle, put one foot in front of the other, or even form a thought? Your body does all this for you—and about a thousand other things at the exact same time—without you ever thinking about it. To perform all these various functions all day, every day, the body-machine requires fuel—lots of it.

So before we move on to our next section, stop being emotional about food. I know we've always placed feelings around what we eat, how we eat, when we eat, and even who cooked it. Mom's apple pie brings back memories of home. Our spouse's favorite dish is a sweet reminder of love in the air. And who doesn't enjoy a little comfort food now and then?

But to crack the fat-loss code and break through your diet plateau forever, you must begin thinking of the body as a machine and the food as fuel. Period, end of story. When we take away the emotions from how we look or what we eat, at least for now, it becomes so much easier to look at fat loss logically.

So remember, food is fuel, and your body is a machine.

	IIIIIIIIIIIII **FAT-LOSS FACT** IIIIIIIIIIIII

Your body needs food to survive. In fact, your body always thinks the last thing you ate is the last thing you'll ever eat.

Perceived Efficiency Rate (PER)

The fuel for our machine comes in the form of the food we eat. So food is our body's fuel, and it is converted to energy to serve the many functions our body must perform each day to survive. Like all good machines, the body must regulate how much energy it uses each day and where its fuel comes from.

How does it do that? You might have heard of the BMR, or basal metabolic rate. Basal metabolic rate is the minimum amount of calories needed to sustain life in a resting individual per day. In other words, this is the amount of energy your body would burn if you were at rest for a full twenty-four hours.

In this book we talk about something called PER, or perceived efficiency rate. What is the PER? PER represents function. Basically, it is the baseline with which your body perceives patterns in your daily activity and your caloric intake and expenditure. It is essentially the amount of calories you need to function on a daily basis at your usual amount of activity. The body, in all of its marvelous, mathematical wizardry, figures out your pattern and can set its baseline accordingly. For instance, say you take a morning walk every day at the same time, pace, and distance. To you, it's exercise. But the body has adapted to the daily routine. To the body, it's just like taking a breath in and a breath out.

Another way to understand it is to take your automobile and fill it with gas. Park it in your driveway, and leave the engine running. Then walk inside, read a book, take a nap, watch the bowl games, do whatever. Come back a few hours later, and the car will have run out of gas.

Even though it didn't go anywhere or travel any miles, your car still burned the fuel you put in it. That's because it was functioning. That full tank of gas allowed your car to idle in the driveway, monitor its systems, and perform a variety of other unseen functions that took place while you were inside reading a book, cheering on your favorite team, or shampooing your hair.

Code Cracker

When your body's in "survival mode," it reserves intake and conserves expenditure.

As goes the car, so goes the body. Even at rest, while you're just sitting there reading this book, your body—a machine built on the need for survival—needs fuel to perform various functions. Pumping blood, keeping your body's temperature where it should be, turning the page, moving your eyes, breathing in and out, monitoring digestion, even sending the electric signals that flick from the page to your brain to increase comprehension—all this requires energy. So even at rest, your body is using fuel. If you forget to feed it, it runs out of gas just as surely as your car idling in the driveway.

So perceived efficiency rate (PER) is that baseline of function that the body thinks it needs to perform those tasks. When you're not giving your body what it needs when it needs it, your body has to survive by calculating on its own how it will take care of itself. When your body's in this "survival mode," it performs two functions:

1. Reserve

2. Conserve

FAT-LOSS FACT

Even at rest, while you're just sitting there reading this book, your body—a machine built on the need for survival—needs fuel to perform various functions.

The Body's Two Functions of Survival

What do these two functions do? And what do they have to do with your diet plateau? The answer to both questions is *plenty*. Let's take a look at what each function is, and then at what it does.

Function 1: Reserve

The first function the body performs in survival mode, after evaluating its PER, the minimum amount of energy it needs to perform all those bodily functions, is to reserve energy. This is an immediate response based on food intake and what the body has in the form of fuel to perform its various functions. Everything your body takes in, in the form of fuel, it immediately sets aside to use for its various functions.

That is why planned eating is so important, and why macro-patterning—regulating how and when you take in protein, fat, and carbohydrates—makes *Crack the Fat-Loss Code* unique. You want to make sure your body gets what it needs when it needs it.

You don't want your body to have to reserve any stores of nutrients, calories, fat, or energy. When the body has what it needs, it performs the way it's supposed to. When you eat haphazardly, starve yourself, defy the laws of nature with the latest fad diet, skip meals, or don't follow a plan, the body will learn to survive on its own. It will reserve the energy you take in.

Like a built-in holding pattern, your body has a system for knowing just how much energy to dole out, and how often. Every seventy-two hours, the body perceives, evaluates, and calculates how much energy you take in and how it can reserve as much of that energy as possible in your body's muscle for later use. Not every day, but every seventy-two hours, your body analyzes the food you take in. You can compare this with your salary. You get paid each month, and you know how much is coming in, and you know what you have going out.

For most of us, this salary stays the same from month to month. Naturally, we come to expect the same amount each month and spend accordingly. If we spend too little, some gets saved. If we spend too much, we have to dip into our savings to cover the loss. If you get stiffed or shorted one week, you definitely know about it. If you get a bonus or work overtime and your paycheck is bigger, you know that, too.

Code Cracker

You want to make sure your body gets what it needs when it needs it.

Your body works the same way. Based on this seventy-two-hour response time, while it is perceiving, evaluating, and calculating your intake, it knows how much it's going to get and adjusts its PER on that amount. When you fluctuate or miss meals or play with its reserves, it responds in kind—but not kindly.

Function 2: Conserve

The body's second function when trying to survive is to conserve energy. In addition to reserving intake, the human body also conserves energy to make sure there is enough energy in the reserves when your body needs it.

I know all of this can sound intimidating at first, but remember: food is fuel, and our body is a machine. So let's put it in terms that fit our comparison. Say you're on the interstate driving, and you see the gas tank is on E, but you look up and notice that the next exit is miles away. How can you make it on an almost-empty tank? What do you do?

Instinctively, you start to conserve energy. You turn off the air to use less gas, roll down the windows, switch off the radio, turn off the cruise control, and drive at a nice, steady pace. You do all that to conserve energy so you can make it to that next gas station and fill your tank back up.

Code Cracker

Much the way your body responds to intake on a seventy-two-hour response time by reserving energy, it responds in a forty-eight-hour cycle by conserving output.

That's just like your body in the conserve mode: it's naturally trying to slow down the processes to conserve energy, so it can complete all its functions. Much the way your body responds to intake on a seventy-two-hour response time by reserving energy, it responds in a forty-eight-hour cycle by conserving output.

If we compare your body's reserve response to the amount of money you have coming in each month, then we can compare its conserve response to the bills you have to pay. Each month you have so much money coming in and so many bills to pay. Based on the amount of your "check" each month (your body's reserves), the conserve function tries to equate money coming in with money going out so that your physical checkbook balances.

Figure 1.1 shows what the 72/48 reserve/conserve function might look like.

FAT-LOSS FACT

Not only does the human body reserve intake, but it also conserves energy to make sure there is enough energy in the reserves when your body needs it.

FIGURE 1.1   Intake and Energy Expenditure

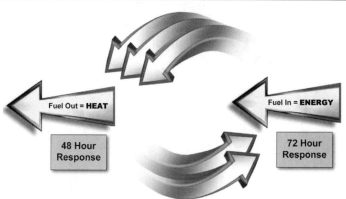

Fuel Out = **HEAT**

Fuel In = **ENERGY**

48 Hour Response

72 Hour Response

The Point of Adaptation

How does the body know what's coming in, what's going out, and how to predict the balance? It turns out that the body is very good at balancing its checkbook. You might even say the body is compulsive about continually monitoring its balance, which is where PER and the 72/48 reserve/conserve response comes in. The body is hypersensitive to its internal balance because the body-machine uses fuel to survive.

Code Cracker

For your body to survive, it has to balance intake and expenditure.

If the body's balance is off, you don't just bounce a check or pay a late fee; your health suffers. The body sees imbalance as a threat to survival. So the stakes are very high for the body. Knowing this may help you understand just why your body always, always fights you when you start a diet. After all, you're stealing money (food) from its balance!

This point where money (energy) in and money (energy) out meets, or balances, is called the point of adaptation. For your body to survive, it has to balance by equating those two functions: reserve and conserve. Adaptation—this constant cycle of perceiving, evaluating, and calculating the body's fuel checkbook—is the body's survival mode. It's also the secret you'll need to crack the fat-loss code.

Code Cracker

If the body's balance is off, you don't just bounce a check or pay a late fee; your health suffers. The body sees imbalance as a threat to survival.

Figure 1.2 describes the body's ongoing quest for survival mode and shows the exact point of adaptation.

The Dieter's Plateau

The dieter's plateau is directly related to the body's adaptive response to food intake (what you eat) and expenditure (the energy your body uses). Think of an internal seesaw, always moving up and down, the body always seeking balance between what it takes in, or intake, and what it uses, or expenditure. Your body, the world's ultimate survival machine, does not want the seesaw sitting in either the upright (intake) or the downturned (expenditure) position for too long. Rather, it seeks balance,

FIGURE 1.2   Understanding the Body's "Survival Mode"

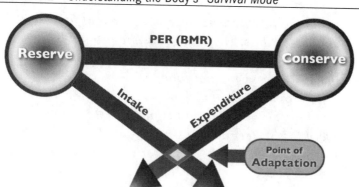

"I Lost Sixteen Pounds in Eight Weeks"

Cathy Marques

In a word, Wendy Chant is a gift! I cannot recommend her or Crack the Fat-Loss Code *highly enough. Her program is the only plan that has ever worked for me as a long-term lifestyle, period. She is truly a lifesaver!*

I am continually impressed with Wendy's passion, knowledge, and mission to spread the truth and teach others the real deal about fitness and weight loss. Her food plans are incredibly easy to follow, and her humor and way of motivating make you want to do a good job.

I promise you, this book will change the way you look at food and eating for the rest of your life. I lost sixteen pounds in eight weeks, all because I met Wendy—and learned to crack the fat-loss code.

and in so doing, it adapts to even out your intake and expenditure columns. This continual monitoring by the body to ensure that the seesaw never stays up or down for too long but instead meets in the middle is known as the body's adaptive response.

In lay terms, the adaptive response is better known as the dieter's "plateau," that dreaded sticking point you reach when the scale doesn't move even after continued attempts to lose weight. Your body is not interested in losing weight; it's interested in keeping as much weight around as it can, so that its task of survival is easier.

FAT-LOSS FACT
It's simply not in your body's best interests to lose weight.

The body's survival depends on how efficient it is at taking care of all its tasks with the only fuel source it has coming in: the food we give it. When you aren't giving your body what it needs, when it needs it, to run efficiently (such as when you start restricting calories or carbs on a "diet"), it kicks into survival mode and tries its best at calculating how it might run better by keeping and holding as many calories as it can. Part of that internal calculation involves shutting down functions such as metabolism to stop expending too much energy.

Maybe now you can see why the dreaded plateau is so common. It's simply not in your body's best interests to lose weight; the more weight it has around, the more fuel it can access to run its everyday bodily functions. The minute you start playing around with that fuel source by restricting calories or a certain type of food, such as carbohydrates or fats, the body must adjust so that it can keep running smoothly.

> ### Code Cracker
> The body's survival depends on how efficient it is at taking care of all of its tasks with the only fuel source it has coming in: the food we give it.

Once your body learns to survive by calculating how to store what you give it and expend less, your diet plateaus. This "sticking point" is failure for the dieter but victory for the body. Your body has won, and you've lost. In fact, now the body has achieved its ultimate task, its purpose for survival.

> ### Code Cracker
> This "sticking point" is failure for the dieter but victory for the body. In fact, now the body has achieved its ultimate task, its purpose for survival.

The Fat-Loss Code

The body's survival mode and adaptive response is the fat-loss code you need to crack so you can lose weight and keep it off for good. Like any code, the "fat-loss code" solves a mystery—in this case, the mystery of why you can restrict calories, lose weight, and then hit the dreaded diet plateau. So cracking the fat-loss code is about understanding the 72/48 adaptive response:

- You've got a body whose job is to survive.
- You've got food coming in: intake.

- You've got energy being used: expenditure.
- You've got a "survival machine" analyzing the fuel coming in every seventy-two hours.
- You've got the same survival machine processing the energy going out every forty-eight hours.
- You've got a point of adaptation where the body analyzes the 72/48 fat-loss code and realizes how much to spend with what's come in.
- And you? You've got a nasty dieter's plateau just waiting to be conquered!

As a result of these very powerful elements, cracking the fat-loss code is a scientific process of macro-patterning during a proven eight-week period specifically designed to counteract the body's inherent adaptive response.

In later chapters of the book, we will discuss each of the eight weeks, going into more detail about the three types of days you'll rotate, including your Food Passes. What's important to remember for right now is that *Crack the Fat-Loss Code* finally gives you the tools you need to understand your body's adaptive response.

Once you know the code, it becomes so simple to eat what you want, when you want, and where you want—for life!

2

Not All Foods
Are Created Equal

How Your Body Uses Fuel

To survive, your body needs fuel, and lots of it. I like to think of this as Private First Class, or PFC. PFC is not a rank, but a simple way for us to understand the very complicated function of macronutrients—otherwise known as *protein*, *fats*, and *carbohydrates*—in your body.

All foods are categorized by what macronutrient is most prominent in their chemical makeup. For example, a large, whole egg has 6 grams of protein, 3 grams of fat, and less than 1 gram of carbohydrates. So eggs are, technically speaking, classified as a protein, even though they do contain some fat and carbohydrates.

Code Cracker
PFC is more than just fuel; it is specific types of fuel for specific types of your body's needs.

Returning to our car analogy from Chapter 1, PFC is more than just fuel; it is specific types of fuel for specific types of your body's needs. After all, you need more than just gas to make your car run; you need oil and coolant as well. That's where PFC comes in:

> **P for Proteins:** Proteins are like gas to your automobile. Protein makes the body go.
> **F for Fats:** Fat is like the oil in your car. Fats keep the body's parts lubricated and your immune function strong.
> **C for Carbohydrates:** Carbohydrates are like coolant to your automobile. They hydrate the body in the absence of water.

Protein

If we compare the body to a car, why is protein like fuel for that car? The reason is that protein is essential for maintenance, repair, and growth of all body tissue. Without body tissue, your body would literally be a motionless bag of bones.

In your diet, proteins are meats, poultry, eggs, fish, and some dairy products. Like gas for your car, they become the fuel that makes your body go. If carbohydrates act like the body's coolant and fats like its oil, then where would your body be without protein? That's right: without the fuel, your car couldn't go anywhere.

Protein is the only macronutrient that supports lean mass in the body, otherwise known as muscle, bone, and structure. These are the building blocks of health. The sturdier your lean mass is, the more structure and mobility your body has overall. The eating program in *Crack the Fat-Loss Code* feeds your lean mass, not your fat.

Six Facts About Fueling Your Body with Protein

We've all heard a lot about protein lately, thanks to popular protein-heavy, low-carb diets. But what is fact, and what is fiction? What is myth, and what is reality? To cut through the fat, so to speak, and better understand the role of protein in the body, here are six facts about fueling your body-machine with protein:

Fact #1: Protein Is Responsible for Muscle Maintenance, Repair, and Growth

You may think the body responds to food willy-nilly, just taking it in and spreading it out. But nothing could be further from the truth. There is a very specific order in which your food is used, and the body naturally responds differently to protein, fats, and carbohydrates.

Earlier on, I said protein is essential for maintenance, repair, and growth of all body tissue, and that's just the order in which your body uses protein. The first amount of protein you take in goes to maintenance, to support muscle and body functions. Throughout the day, our bodies perform routine duties that create wear and tear on muscles and joints. The soreness in your legs after jogging or the ache in the balls of your feet after standing in line at the DMV for a few hours—these and so many more instances of the body's wear and tear require maintenance so we can use these various parts again tomorrow.

Code Cracker

I like to say that life is ballistic. The body is always breaking itself down to build itself back up.

Next, your body uses protein for repair. I like to say that life is ballistic. The body is always breaking itself down to build itself back up. Trainers tell you that you're building muscle when you lift weights, but what you're really doing is ballistic; you're actually tearing down muscle tissue, not building it up. How does the body repair torn or worn muscle tissue? Through protein, of course.

Finally, protein is used to promote the body's growth. We often think protein grows only muscles, but other types of growth occur thanks to protein as well. Protein is the major source of building material for muscle, blood, skin, hair, nails, and internal organs. It is needed for formation of hormones, including testosterone; enzymes, which are substances necessary for basic life functions; and antibodies, which help resist foreign substances in the body.

Fact #2: Protein Burns More Calories

Did you know that protein can literally heat up your metabolism? That's right. Protein has something known as thermic effect of food (TEF). This TEF is 0.25 times the total number of protein calories ingested. In contrast, carbohydrates and fat have a TEF of only 0.04 to 0.06 expenditure of total calories ingested. That means protein ingestion burns 36 percent more energy than carbs and fats.

In other words, you can count on burning up to five times as many calories when you eat protein as when you eat the other two macronutrients. So how do fat and carbs stack up? See for yourself: For every 500 calories of protein you take in, you expend 125 calories through protein's thermic effect. Carbohydrates and fat, through their thermic effect, each burn a measly 30 calories per 500 eaten.

Fact #3: An Active Person's Body Needs 1 Gram of Protein for Every Pound of Lean Body Weight

You should consume 1 gram of protein for every pound of lean mass you weigh. For example, if you weigh 160 pounds and have 30 percent body fat, your lean mass is 112 pounds. In this case, you should consume about 112 grams of protein total each day, spread over five to six meals.

It's important to consume just enough protein, and not too little or not too much. How much protein is enough? When is there such a thing as too much protein?

What's adequate for a woman is 3 to 4 ounces at any given meal. Men, on the other hand, should consume 6 to 8 ounces of protein at any one meal. Above and beyond that amount is excess to the body. Why is it dangerous to eat excessive amounts of protein? After all, we've just seen how great it is for your body's metabolism. Well, too much protein at one time is counterproductive; the body can't use it all at once, so the rest goes to the kidneys for processing, and the spillover gets broken down into fat.

Code Cracker

If we follow modern American trends, we're getting double and triple portions!

Even protein, when you eat too much, can turn to fat. So eat protein throughout your day, but be careful to eat it in proper portions. Portion size can be a real problem, especially if you eat out a lot. If you look at the ounces listed next to your favorite serving of steak, chicken, or even fish, you'll see that 10 or 12 ounces is the norm, not the exception. If 3 to 4 ounces for women and 6 to 8 ounces for men is the ideal, then it's clear to see that if we follow modern American trends, we're getting double and triple portions! Embrace the benefits of quality protein, but since we know excess protein eventually gets processed in the kidneys and turned into fat, be sure to watch your portion sizes carefully.

Fact #4: Protein Helps You Maintain a Positive Nitrogen Balance Around the Clock

Nitrogen balance is not just important; it's *all*-important. What is nitrogen, and why is it so important? Simply put, nitrogen is a by-product of protein's breakdown in the body. Much as your car uses gas and emits exhaust from the tailpipe, the body also produces a by-product whenever it uses protein.

Nitrogen is literally the thing that makes your muscles hard and firm—not weight training, but nitrogen. When the nitrogen level in your muscle has a positive balance, your muscles are firm, harder, and healthier. When muscle has a negative balance, because of poor protein intake, your muscle is unhealthy, or what I like to think of as "squishy." When your muscle is unhealthy, your body is more likely to use it for energy, which is the last thing you want.

Another way to think of nitrogen balance is to picture a hollow PVC pipe. With a negative nitrogen balance, that PVC pipe is flimsy and hollow; maybe it weighs ten pounds. Fill the pipe with concrete (muscle), and now it weighs fifteen pounds. The pipe hasn't changed shape or gotten bigger, but it has gotten heavier, because muscle does weigh more than fat.

I repeat: muscle weighs more than fat. For many years, we have been concerned with our weight, to the detriment of our shape. Many of my clients confess that they weigh themselves religiously, once or twice—or more—a day. But the fact that muscle weighs more than fat flies in the face of those religious scale watchers.

That's why this book is called *Crack the Fat-Loss Code* and not *Crack the Weight-Loss Code*. I urge you to be more concerned with your shape than with your weight. For example, you can trust a handy pair of jeans or slacks that fit better as you lose fat, rather than a scale that doesn't differentiate between weight and fat.

> **Code Cracker**
> Don't use a scale to measure your progress.
> Instead, use a pair of pants or slacks that fit
> when you had less body fat.

Having a positive nitrogen net balance is all-important, because it builds healthy muscle. When the muscle is healthy, the body won't turn to muscle for energy, because it's harder to burn. It will turn to fat instead, because, as always, the body follows the path of least resistance. When we build firm, healthy muscle, we make it harder for the body to tap muscle for energy use. Don't make it easier for your body to rob muscle for energy; create a positive nitrogen balance, and make it harder.

Fact #5: You Need Quality Proteins at Each Meal

Unlike carbohydrates, which are quickly utilized and almost immediately processed for energy, protein doesn't last throughout the day. As a result, you have to keep taking in quality proteins throughout the day. Otherwise, the body will want to shed poor muscle tissue instead of fat.

But not all proteins are created equal. In fact, proteins are rated on a scientific scale that measures something called their BV/PU biovalue, based on protein utilization. Like most rating systems, proteins are rated as to their biovalue in a descending scale, starting with the most "biologically valuable" foods at the top.

> **Code Cracker**
> Not all proteins are created equal; they're
> rated by BV/PU.

Hands down, the protein biovalue winner is the egg. Nature's number-one protein source, eggs are the highest-quality protein "for the cluck." They have 100 percent biovalue. That means that when you eat eggs, 100 percent can be used by the body toward a positive nitrogen balance for maintenance, repair, and growth of the muscle. Beef, poultry, and fish are in the ninetieth percentile; dairy products range in the eightieth percentile. Pork is one of the poorest biovalues of any protein; it's in the 60th percentile range. (I consider that a failing grade, wouldn't you?)

Fact #6: Eating Protein Helps You Burn Fat

Protein promotes a glucagon response in your human body-machine. I like to call glucagon your fat-burning hormone potion; it aids us in releasing and unlocking fat by making it usable for the body. As you take in protein, you're increasing glucagon levels.

Exercise is another way to increase glucagon, but the only food responsible for this great fat-burning hormone potion is *protein*. That's important to the fat-loss code, because it counteracts the body's hypoglycemic effect, an important factor in how your body uses—and stores—fat. So don't think protein; think your fat-burning hormone potion!

FAT-LOSS FACT

Protein is essential for growth and maintenance of all body tissue.

Fats

Inside your body-machine, fats are the oil that lubricates the many systems needed to get you through your day. Fats include butter, margarine, oils, nuts, and seeds. Like proteins and carbohydrates, fats are a fairly complicated, very complex concept. There are four types of fat:

1. *Polyunsaturated fats:* nuts and seeds

2. *Monounsaturated fats:* oils

3. *Saturated fat:* solids

4. *Trans-fatty acids:* hydrogenated

Fat has gotten a bad rap lately. The truth is that we need fat in our diets. The main functions of fats are important:

- Providing fuel; fatty acids are a major fuel source during exercise
- Providing insulation
- Aiding in absorption of fat-soluble vitamins
- Acting as an energy storehouse
- Supplying essential fatty acids
- Providing protective padding for body structures and organs
- Serving as a component of all cell membranes and other cell structures
- Supplying building blocks for other biomolecules

Like oil in your car, fat doesn't get used quite as often as protein (gas). This is a great way to think of fat in the diet. We need it, just not so much of it.

Unsaturated Fats: Polyunsaturated and Monounsaturated

Like proteins, not all fats are created equal. The more natural a fat is, the more healthful and less harmful it is for you. The most healthful fats are polyunsaturated and monounsaturated fats. These are mostly found in natural foods: nuts and seeds for polyunsaturated fats, and oils for monounsaturated fats.

Nuts are a great natural food, brimming with polyunsaturated fat to oil and lubricate your body-machine. As most of us know, however, nuts are calorie-dense. So while nuts are a good-quality fat—and it's all about the quality of your fats—they can also offset your other positive health initiatives by taking up much of your day's daily calorie allotment. So enjoy nuts, but be careful to avoid eating too many, too often.

The same goes for oils. Be careful to use healthful oils such as olive oil, flaxseed oil, and fish oil, but do so in moderation. According to recent studies, flaxseed can cause prostate enlargement in men, so men should avoid flaxseed oil.

Even when having a salad, we can undo all the positive health benefits of fresh vegetables, fruits, and nuts by dousing it with too much oil. So as you do with nuts, use oil, but use it sparingly.

Saturated Fats

Saturated fat is solid at room temperature and is generally found in meat and processed foods. Studies have shown that too much saturated fat in the diet raises the cholesterol level in the blood-stream. Reducing saturated fats is a good idea, especially for individuals with excessive body fat and individuals with high cholesterol.

Trans-Fatty Acids

We hear a lot about trans-fatty acids these days. Trans fats are formed when unsaturated vegetable fat is altered by adding hydrogen atoms, creating a type of fat that did not exist in nature. After this process, the fat molecule is said to be "hydrogenated." The problem with trans-fatty acids is that your body doesn't know what to do with them.

Hydrogenation transforms the shape of a fatty acid to a "trans" form. This molecule does not occur in nature, and the body has difficulty digesting it. This is the problem with margarine—it contains hydrogenated, trans-fatty acids. Hydrogenated fat is also commonly associated with junk food: potato chips, cookies, etc.

Trans-fatty acids may help preserve food so that it tastes good, but your body can't break them down and use them correctly. Normal fats are very supple and pliable, but the trans-fatty acid is a stiff fat that can build up in the body and create havoc.

The areas affected include the lining of your blood vessels and brain surfaces, where the buildup can cause dysfunction. Studies show this type of molecule to be more associated with artery disease than the saturated ("hard") fat found in butter. Trans-fatty acids are linked to obesity, heart disease, diabetes, high cholesterol, and even sudden cardiac death.

If that's not enough to give you pause next time you double your order of fries or take a bite of artificial cheese pizza, consider that the chemical recipe for a trans-fatty acid involves putting hydrogen atoms (thus that *hydrogenated* term you see) in the "wrong" place. It's like making a plastic.

And who would want to eat plastic?

FAT-LOSS FACT

Trans-fatty acids may help preserve food so that it tastes good, but your body can't break them down and use them correctly.

Eat Quality Fats

In avoiding fat, be careful that you don't eliminate fat, even saturated fat. After all, just because something has saturated fat doesn't mean it's necessarily bad. Too often people brag about how they eat only egg whites and leave out the yolk, but for the body's purposes, this is like throwing out the baby with the bathwater. A yolk and an egg white work together and have important nutrients. A single egg yolk is not going to make your cholesterol go out of whack, so remember to treat food logically, not emotionally. Be careful to avoid the hype and do your own research. If a new study comes out about the effects of eggs, or yolks, or saturated fat, or cholesterol, don't just stop at the headline, but read the entire report. It's good for you!

> ### Code Cracker
> Fats are an important part of the diet, but don't go to extremes. Too much or too little is an extreme; we want a balance.

When it comes to fat, it all comes down to quality. You need fat because it protects your immune system and lubricates the body's parts. It also aids in the digestion of food and keeps your immune system—the body's army—fit and ready to do battle against sickness and disease.

Fats are an important part of the diet, but don't go to extremes. Too much or too little is an extreme; we want a balance. Use fats wisely. Think about what you're putting on your food.

Too much fat, even good fat, will make you fat. Fat has the largest amount of calories of all food categories. So if you eat too many fats or consume processed food that contains added fat, some of that food energy is likely to be left unused and put aside as fat.

Carbohydrates

Carbohydrates have also gotten a bad rap these days. In many ways, the carbohydrate is the orphan of the macronutrient family. People spend so much time talking up protein and talking down fat that poor little carbohydrates get the short end of the nutritional stick.

Despite the prevalence of "low-carb" diets—and the way they are perceived as successful by many short-term dieters—carbohydrates are actually vital to the human body. The primary function of carbohydrates is for energy usage and storage. Carbohydrates can also be used as a coolant for the human machine, making carbs a fast-acting, energy-releasing macronutrient that will prove integral to cracking the fat-loss code in the next section. This largest of all food groups includes grains, bread, pasta, potatoes, vegetables, fruits, sweets, and alcohol.

Why do we compare carbohydrates with coolant? It's because carbohydrates provide hydration to the body when water consumption is not optimal. The word *carbohydrate* literally means a kind of compound made "with water." *Carbo* refers to the carbon atoms in carbohydrates; *hydrate* means they are combined with water.

The body chooses carbohydrates for energy because they digest first and most easily. Sensory receptors on the tongue respond almost immediately to the presence of carbohydrates. As soon as the carb hits the mouth, it can begin breaking down.

Code Cracker

Carbs elicit the release of the hormone serotonin, otherwise known as the "feel good" hormone.

When we speak of food creating an emotional response, carbohydrates are at the top of the list. That is because carbs elicit the release of the hormone serotonin, otherwise known as the "feel good" hormone. When you think of comfort foods—pasta, mashed potatoes, macaroni and cheese—think of carbohydrates and that "feel good" hormonal response.

Carbohydrates are also known for affecting your blood sugar, because they promote an insulin response. I'll discuss this more in Chapter 3.

FAT-LOSS FACT

The body chooses carbohydrates for energy because they digest first and most easily.

How Your Body Uses—and Stores—Energy and Excess Fat from Carbohydrates

Let's not treat carbohydrates like orphans anymore. In fact, when it comes to cracking the fat-loss code, carbohydrates are your friend. By manipulating all of the macronutrients in our macro-patterning program, particularly carbohydrates, we train your body to use fat and the carbohydrates we eat for energy instead of shuttling them off to fat stores immediately, the way it does in most cases when you're not eating properly. So when you learn more about carbohydrates, when to eat them, and how much, you are that much closer to breaking through your dieting plateau forever.

The true education about carbohydrates is well overdue. Not only are carbs some of our favorite foods, but they have important functions in the body. As mentioned, they promote the release of our "feel good" hormone, serotonin. They are also responsible for the output of our thyroid hormones, which in turn keep our metabolism running. Once you understand that carbs are good— and good for you—you will be happy not to have to give up your favorite foods or stop eating "the white stuff" any longer.

Your body uses carbohydrates in stages that determine use for immediate energy, stored energy, or stored fat. Carbohydrates' quick digestion and immediate availability make them the body's first choice for energy usage and storage. Let's discover how your body uses energy from carbohydrates and stores the excess as fat in these three different stages.

Stage 1: Immediate Energy Needs

When the body needs energy, it doesn't want to mess around with auditioning new sources of energy. It wants a go-to macronutrient for fast, effective, and "immediate" energy. The body's go-to source for energy is carbohydrates. That's because there's no waiting around. Carbs are immediately available for energy—something the body loves about them! Digestion begins in the mouth, and carbohydrates are quickly made available for energy needs or stored for later use.

Stage 2: Storage in the Muscle and Liver

While the digestion of carbohydrates starts immediately in the mouth, the rest of that digestion continues in the small intestine. The energy that isn't used immediately by the body goes to the same place as everything else you can't use right away but know you're going to need pretty soon: straight to storage.

Your body stores carbohydrates as glycogen in the muscle and liver as a source of energy for movement and daily function. The human body is an expert at knowing what to store, how much, where, and when. The amount of these stores equates to the amount of muscle on one's body, and stores continue until the muscle and/or liver is full from too much carbohydrate consumption and not enough exercise.

Throughout the day, when food is not present or when we're not feeding our body the right kinds of food—as is the case when we are on a high-protein, low-carb diet or the body is taking in massive amounts of quick, fried, zapped, or fake foods—the body wants to be able to go into storage and take out the energy it needs.

Stage 3: Storing Fat/Spillover

Centuries ago, when men and women were constantly active, hunting and gathering and finding and foraging for daily food, the third stage didn't really apply. From day to day, cavemen and -women were lucky to get enough to eat, let alone eat too much. At times when the hunters were fortunate enough to kill a big woolly mammoth, they had no choice but to eat the whole animal and stuff themselves until the next big kill.

They ate what they could; they overate. They stuffed themselves, and the body responded. That excess energy had to go somewhere, so it became fat. Today we are in a continual stage of abundance. We can eat as many woolly mammoth burgers as we like, all day long if we want.

For perhaps the first time in history, we are eating far too much, far too often. It's not hard to do anymore, and it's not always purposeful. Look at portion sizes. In an effort to beat out the competition, many restaurants are serving more food for less money. This means bigger steaks, sometimes twelve to fourteen ounces! This means two breasts of chicken instead of one. This means bigger bagels, more cream cheese, larger side orders, and bigger cones in which to fit more scoops of ice cream.

Likewise, we move less—and less often—than ever before. We drive here; we drive there. We drive all morning to get to a job where we sit all day before getting in the car and driving home to sit some more. Maybe we stop by the gym a few times a week. Maybe our schedule is too busy to allow even that.

More food—or "energy," as the body perceives it—and less movement means more energy and nowhere for it to go. All of that excess food, plus the energy left over from our sedentary lifestyles, has to go somewhere. When energy intake is continually abundant with little or no expenditure of that energy (that is, when you eat more and move less), muscle and liver stores overfill, and your body stores excess, unused energy as fat.

How to Make Fat Your Go-to Energy Source

So why is it important that you know one of these stages, let alone all three? It's because the way your body stores energy is the same way it uses it. Understanding the fat-loss code is all about understanding how the human body—Mother Nature's most reliable survival machine—works. What makes it tick? How do the systems work with, or against, one another? How does doing *this* affect *that*, and why?

Code Cracker

Your body is too important to treat like some used car with no spare tire in the trunk.

So many of us treat our bodies the way we do our cars, driving them as hard and as fast as we can. We choose the cheapest (processed, fried) and most convenient (fast, junk) fuel until our bodies literally break down (obesity, stress, fatigue) and we have to take them into the shop (doctor's office, diet book, gym).

Your body is too important to treat like some used car with no spare tire in the trunk. And as strong as it is—your body is, after all, the ultimate survivor—it's also very delicate. If you feed it poorly enough for long enough, your health suffers.

Your Body, the Perfect Square

Over the years, the human body has been represented by many shapes and sizes: the pear, the oval, the circle, the straight line, the image of perfection. When we talk about the body at ForeverFit, we say, "Be there, be square."

To me, the square is the epitome of the perfect body shape. Not because a square is better than a pear shape or a circle, but because the square symbolizes balance in all things: four equal sides creating a shape that is impervious to disease or poor health.

As you look at Figure 2.1, you see the square outlined as the perfect body shape. Next to it, where you see the fat attached to the square, the figure looks out of shape, just as body fat takes your body out of shape. So when I talk about "staying in shape,"

FIGURE 2.1   Fat Attached to Body

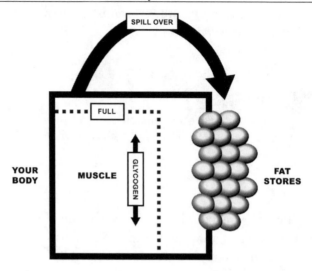

unlike most trainers, I'm talking about keeping the body in balance with the system I introduce in *Crack the Fat-Loss Code*.

To keep your body from taking on the wrong shape, we need to look at how the body can get out of alignment. That happens when it responds to too much food, the wrong kinds of food, the wrong times of food, and even not enough food with an adaptive response that makes your body look anything but square.

Since the body is a square and loves balance on all of its sides, we must strive hard to train the body *not* to store too much of this spillover as fat. In the same way that the body is in a continual 72/48 reserve/conserve response (the basis for the code), we too must be vigilant in what we eat and when we eat, so the body never has too much to store and upset our perfect square.

By now you know I love comparisons, and since I recognize that the understanding of how the body uses food is challenging to understand at first, I have a great way of comparing the body's use of food to a calculator.

When you eat food, your body uses it as fuel. But fuel is worthless if the body can't tap into some of it *now*, some of it *later*, and some *in case of emergency*. Fortunately, when you eat, the body has the ability to tap into what you eat for energy.

Like most machines, your body seeks the path of least resistance. That's why carbohydrates are your body's first choice for its main source of energy: they digest first, and then the body also makes them readily available or stores them for later use.

Code Cracker

Glycogen stored in the muscle is the body's "battery pack."

The body's muscles can be likened to its internal storage shed; what it stores there is glycogen. When we talk about glycogen, this is just a fancy word for stored energy from carbohydrate consumption. So as we have seen, energy is either used right away or stored as glycogen while the extra spills over into fat, which is why there is a fat-loss code to crack in the first place.

The way your body uses energy is interesting: When you're not feeding yourself, the body is still functioning. So where does it get its energy even when you're not scarfing down proteins, carbohydrates, or fats? Well, here is where we return to our electric calculator, which like the body has three energy sources: a plug that goes into the wall, a battery backup, and if all else fails and there is no wall to plug it into or the batteries go bad, a solar panel strip that serves as a kind of backup generator.

Here is how the body-machine-calculator breaks down:

• **Electricity:** The juice the calculator gets from being plugged directly into the wall can be compared to the instant

"I Found Wendy Just in Time"

Jenny Young

I have been overweight my entire life. Like many women, I have tried and struggled and watched my weight fluctuate since I was a teen. About five years ago, I decided to begin to replace my bad habits with healthy ones. This was a wonderful decision for me in so many ways, but believe it or not, my weight problem still didn't get any abetter.

Then I met Wendy Chant. We met by accident about ten months ago. I was very skeptical at first, but Wendy disarmed me with her knowledge and down-to-earth manner the first time I heard her speak. In the time she has worked with me, Wendy has taught me to take the principles of health in general and focus them specifically toward fat loss.

Crack the Fat-Loss Code is one of the best things that has ever happened to me—everything

Wendy has taught me has worked! I have lost over forty pounds since my first class and now have only about twenty pounds left to reach my goal. (I haven't been this small since elementary school!)

I am looking toned, too, and my recent doctor's appointment found me to be "ridiculously healthy." I am complimented constantly, and I feel great—not just about how I look, but also about how I am living. I love this program. I love how much sense it makes, how well it works, and how it gives me a wonderful balance of eating healthy and indulging in my favorite things. Since I understand the struggle of weight loss, I wish for everyone who has that struggle that they could stumble upon this program.

energy the body gets from absorbing carbohydrates, the digestion of which begins on the tongue, for quick-source fuel.

• **Batteries:** So what happens if you're not eating and still need fuel? Well, that can be likened to your needing to use your calculator when there is no electrical outlet available. You can still add with it (use electricity), because there is a battery pack for just such an occasion. In the body, this battery pack is the glycogen stored in the body's muscles. With no direct fuel source to pull from—no food being eaten—the body will call on this glycogen second to satisfy its energy needs. So the glycogen stored in the muscle is the body's battery pack.

• **Solar panel:** So what happens if you have no electricity available for your calculator *and* the backup batteries go dead? Guess what; you can *still* use that calculator, and for quite some time, because the emergency default is located on that handy little solar panel at the top of your calculator. How does this match up in the human body? Here is why it's so important to crack the fat-loss code: as a means of last resort, only *after* the body has used the direct fuel from the food you eat or stored fuel from the glycogen in your muscles, it will then, and only then, use the fat stored in your fat cells for energy.

Code Cracker

The body's muscles can be likened to its internal storage shed. What it stores there is glycogen. When we talk about glycogen, this is just a fancy word for stored energy from carbohydrate consumption.

So as we can see, for the body to break down fat and actually start using it as energy, we have to burn through not only the food you eat four to six times a day but also the glycogen stored away in the body's muscles. We have to try running only on solar power, our backup energy source. When you crack the fat-loss code, losing fat is as easy as adding on your calculator.

Fortunately, I have designed an eight-week program to do just that.

PART 2

Crack the
Fat-Loss Code

3

Efficient Fat Loss and Optimal Health

Five Keys to Success

The 72/48 reserve/conserve code is how the body survives by adapting to the stressors placed upon it through life's journey. It perceives, evaluates, and calculates continually the energy intake and expenditure it will need and use daily for its survival. Through these adaptive abilities, the body achieves its survival goals.

Unfortunately, survival and healthy living are not necessarily the same thing. Good health means all functions of the body are working as they should, so that body fat is at a healthy level, the immune functions are working well, energy levels are high, and stress is managed properly. Good health is living. Survival is just the means of the body keeping enough of its vital systems running. Survival is just existing.

FAT-LOSS FACT

Our energy expenditure is intimately linked to our energy intake.

The human body is a complex network of chemical, hormonal, and biological interactions that contribute to the body's ability to perceive, evaluate, and calculate energy intake and expenditure. Our energy expenditure is intimately linked to our energy intake. By understanding this integration of intake and expenditure, we hope to find ways to dissociate the relationship.

For example, if expenditure weren't so dependent on intake, we could more easily manipulate our body composition by avoiding that nasty metabolic shutdown that accompanies dieting. Conversely, if expenditure didn't send such strong signals that stimulate our urge to eat, we would all go hungry. When out of control or in extreme cases, these signals can cause food addictions and eating disorders. Balance of these signals is optimal in your quest for a healthy body and great appearance.

That's where *Crack the Fat-Loss Code* comes in. By controlling our body's signals rather than the other way around, we not only short-circuit its power of adaptation, but do so in a way that makes us feel full instead of starving as if we were on a diet.

Code Cracker

Crack the Fat-Loss Code takes the mystery out of your body, a machine that literally fights every effort you make to lose fat.

Most popular diets today don't talk about the plateau. The real reason most diets don't talk about the dieter's plateau is that it's inevitable. Instead, they focus on just one weight-loss key. They put the emphasis on "eating less" by raving about exercise, or they concentrate on regulating "blood sugar" because they know you'll at least see results that way. But what they're missing is the body's ultimate desire to survive through the adaptive response.

If you don't talk about the adaptive response, that doesn't mean it's going to go away; it just means your diet won't be long-lasting. This part of the book doesn't talk about one key, or even two keys. Instead, I talk about five keys for efficiently overcoming the adaptive response so you can burn fat and achieve optimal health.

Being healthy is more important now than ever before. Did you know that a baby girl born in 2010 may live to be 120 years old? These days we are living longer than ever. But are we really living *better*?

When I talk about fat loss, I do it from a health perspective. Remember, we are looking at fat loss logically, not emotionally. Food is fuel, and the body is a machine; that is all we are concerned with (for now). Certainly, your appearance is important, but a healthy life is more important than an attractive life.

FAT-LOSS FACT

Your body adapts, and the only way to achieve sustainable fat loss is to perform efficient fat loss.

Fat loss is the same process for everyone. Your body needs to be efficient at the process. It has something to do with metabolic rate, to be sure, but losing fat efficiently is more important than changing your metabolism to speed up the fat-loss process. To concentrate on only one part of the process, such as speeding up metabolism or eliminating one of the PFC, is to short-circuit the process and render it useless.

There are five simple keys for achieving efficient fat loss and optimal health:

1. Protect and support muscle.

2. Level blood sugar.

3. Create an energy deficit.

4. Produce heat.

5. Manipulate energy stores.

Think of the five keys to optimal health as a fine cup of coffee, and of your body (the machine) as a coffeemaker. To brew a fine cup of coffee, you have to follow all of the steps for the coffeemaker. You must pour the water, fill the filter, replace the filter, close the lid, put the carafe on the burner, plug it in, and push the "on" button.

If any of these essential elements are left out—if you forget to put coffee in the filter or even the right amount of scoops of coffee in the filter, if you forget to put the carafe on the burner or leave it on too long, or if you don't plug in the machine—your coffee could come out weak, burnt, too strong, or even as clear, hot water.

Your body is the same. Optimal fat loss is not only losing fat for the right reasons, but also losing fat efficiently. Anyone can lose fat. Starve yourself, eat only protein, work out six hours a day—all of these ill-advised attempts will have the same result: less fat. But will it stay off? No, because no matter what you do to your body, the ultimate survival machine, it will adapt and find a way to put fat back on as it continually perceives, evaluates, and responds to your fad diet of the month.

That is why fad diets don't work—and dieters reach a plateau. Your body adapts, and the only way to achieve sustainable fat loss is to perform effective and efficient fat loss.

And that's what cracking the fat-loss code is all about!

 FAT-LOSS FACT
Optimal fat loss is not only losing fat for the right reasons, but also losing fat efficiently.

Key 1: Protect and Support Muscle

It may seem odd that our first key to efficient fat loss and optimal health involves muscle. But muscle is so important to cracking the fat-loss code. And here's why: Our muscles support and hold us up. Without them, we would literally just be a bag of bones lying flat. We rely on muscle for support, strength, and stamina.

Our bodies, however, don't like muscle. Much as the body thinks of a diet as a battle cry to reserve and conserve energy, so it considers muscle a liability. For every pound of muscle on your body, you burn twenty to thirty calories in the course of a day without activity. For every pound of fat, you burn just four to five calories. In other words, with more muscle, you burn more calories, which is bad for the energy-hording body but great for the dieter.

So since you burn more calories with more muscle, when there is an energy deficit, your body would rather shed muscle as its first source of energy. But it can't do so if the muscle is protected. That's why it's so vital for us to protect and support muscle.

The only way to get your body to burn fat instead of muscle is to make it easier for the body to do so. Remember, your body wants it clean and easy. The easier we can make it for your body to go grab fat, the more likely it is to do so.

When your body has more muscle, you gain a host of new benefits. For starters, you have a firmer, more toned appearance. You also create and have more room to store glycogen, because your internal energy reservoir is bigger. Muscle also protects the bone and makes you less likely to develop osteoporosis.

Our job is to keep the body working harder, to make it go look for energy somewhere other than your muscle. Unfortunately, the popular media and diet industry have told you that starvation is the answer. But it's not.

Code Cracker

By protecting and supporting our muscle, and never skipping meals, we train the body to look elsewhere for its energy source.

Think of it this way: You get up in the morning and are already behind the eight ball. There are the kids to feed, never mind yourself. You've got errands to run, the kids to drop off, prescriptions to fill, dry-cleaning to pick up—and, oh yeah, the gym to run to. By the time you get to the gym, you're walking into your daily workout around ten or eleven—with no food.

Now your body needs energy. Where will it look first? That's right; your muscle. Working out with no food source as energy sends your body scrambling to break something down quickly and use it as an energy source. Your body is literally breaking down muscle to get some energy for your workout!

By protecting and supporting our muscle, and never skipping meals, we train the body to look elsewhere for its energy source. Strong, healthy muscles help you burn energy and protect your body. Using the other four keys I introduce here, we help train your body to use fat and the food we take in.

Key 1 is a two-prong process: First, we protect muscle by exercising with resistance training. Second, we support muscle by eating the proper foods for muscle maintenance, repair, and growth, which we've learned are proteins such as meat, poultry, and eggs.

For example, if you lifted fifty-gallon drums every day for work and then stopped doing it just for a few weeks, it would be hard for you to go back and lift those drums again. Your body had needed the muscle to lift them, but as soon as it didn't, your body did its best to get rid of that muscle, because it wasn't needed.

FAT-LOSS FACT

For every pound of muscle on your body, you
burn twenty to thirty calories. For every pound
of fat, you burn just four to five calories, or a
fraction of the energy needed by the body's
precious reserves.

Key 2: Level Blood Sugar

The second adaptive response to manipulate is the understanding of balanced blood sugar levels. Increased levels of blood
sugar promote fat storage; balanced blood sugar levels make the
body capable of using stored fatty acids as a source of energy.
More fibrous carbohydrates and fewer days of sugary carb consumption will promote a better balance of blood sugar. A diet
containing only low-carb foods is hard to live long-term, and
most people will eventually abandon these types of plans.

We hear a lot about low blood sugar (hypoglycemia) and
high blood sugar (diabetes). Neither high nor low blood sugar is
optimum for the human body, let alone fat loss. We are looking
for level blood sugar—balanced blood sugar levels that are not
too high and not too low.

To understand food and how it affects your blood sugar, it's
important to understand the glycemic index. The glycemic index
of a certain food or nutrient basically describes how quickly the
body absorbs the sugars found within that food. It does so by
comparing how rapidly carbohydrates are converted to blood
sugar compared with glucose, which is given an index of 100.
The lower the glycemic index, the smaller the glycemic response
to the food eaten.

Foods either absorb quickly, at a relatively high rate, or
slowly, at a low rate. The more quickly a food gets absorbed
(the higher the glycemic index), the more likely it is to be stored
as fat. That's because these readily available sugars send a signal

to your body to release insulin. In turn, insulin sends a message to your fat cells: "Hey, there's too much sugar clogging up the bloodstream. Your fat cells start absorbing all the excess sugar to get it out of your blood system." This is why so-called "white foods" get a bad name. White potatoes, white rice, and white bread are all good examples of foods with high glycemic indexes. Their quick, almost immediate absorption in your body leads to those insulin signals to store the excess sugar as fat.

Generally speaking, it is wise to choose foods with a low glycemic index (especially if they are to be eaten alone) in order to achieve sustained energy and appetite control. But we want to enjoy life; a big part of that is eating various foods. I wouldn't design a meal plan so full of absolutes that you could "never" enjoy a Chinese dinner out with your friends and partake of white rice and hot tea with sugar. I wouldn't say to a client, "You'll never be able to eat pizza again."

That is not living; this is "dieting for a living." *Crack the Fat-Loss Code* is not about a diet; it's about a lifestyle.

Three factors regulate your blood sugar:

1. **Food item:** The item is what you take in. Too many of the wrong carbohydrates create high blood sugar, while not enough can produce low blood sugar.

2. **Timing:** This is how often you eat. Avoid going too long between meals. Long gaps of no eating signal the body to raise blood sugar on its own.

3. **Amount:** Finally, the amount of food matters. Big meals create a rise in blood sugar. Even when no carbohydrates are present, your body will release insulin to deal with the overload of food.

Don't worry; I leave none of this to chance. You'll find that your meal plan takes in all of these factors. Not just for the first eight weeks, but forever. Once you learn how to macro-pattern for life, it truly does take all the guesswork out of regulating your blood sugar levels.

Code Cracker

Neither high nor low blood sugar is optimum for the human body. We are looking for level blood sugar, not too high and not too low.

Key 3: Create an Energy Deficit

The third step for the efficiency of fat loss and optimal health is creating an energy deficit. In other words, you can't crack the fat-loss code without a reason for your body to go get that excess fat you have stored.

Think of it this way: Your body likes to have energy in the "bank." It's an energy hoarder; it doesn't like to "spend" energy. The safest, surest way for the body to store energy is in the fat cells, so if we don't create an energy deficit, there will always be plenty of fat for the body to store up and save for later. We have to create an energy deficit so that the body dips into its savings account and spends some of that fat.

There are two ways to create an energy deficit: calorie reduction and exercise.

Calorie Reduction

By reducing the amount of calories you eat, you provide less energy for the body to store. It's like docking your body's "fat pay." Last week your body was able to store X amount of energy because you ate five hundred more calories. By reducing calories, the body has less energy to put in storage for rapid use. Where does the body store energy for rapid use? That's right: as glycogen in the muscles.

Where does your body have to go when it needs to dip into savings because there's not enough in the muscles? That's right:

fat! Calorie reduction is one way to force an energy deficit in favor of fatty acids as a source of energy. Unfortunately, the body senses calorie reduction quickly. For those who have used calorie-reduction diets continually, it is almost immediate that the body begins to conserve energy and reduce the metabolic rate.

When we create an energy deficit, the body must look to fat sooner for an energy source. We effectively bypass the quick source of energy in our food as well as the energy stored as glycogen in our muscles. In other words, the body must go grab fat.

We can't be in a constant calorie deficit, because the body will adapt to it. As you'll see in key 5, macro-patterning is important; it stops the adaptive process. By alternating not only the amount of food you eat but also the types of macronutrients, you make sure that the body never gets a chance to adapt.

Exercise

To further counteract the adaptive response, it is important to alternate calorie reduction with the second way of creating an energy deficit: exercise. Exercise also uses energy, so we can create a second type of energy deficit by moving our bodies more actively, more often. Remember that when we talk about creating an energy deficit, we are literally talking about spending our body's precious energy. It doesn't like that!

Think of how you and I spend money. For our daily needs—groceries, bills, meals, gas, entertainment, and so on—we use our checking account. Only when there is an emergency or we need to splurge on a vacation or home improvement do we turn to our savings account.

The body works the same way. So think of the energy (glycogen) we store in our muscles as the body's energy checking account, and the energy we store as fat as the body's savings account. The more we create an energy deficit by reducing calories or increasing exercise, the less there is in the body's checking account. That means it has to go dip into savings and use up some fat for its energy needs.

Exercise has so many benefits, it's important to do some every day. Yet no matter what exercise you do or how often, it's important to keep it varied and change it up from day to day and week to week. Lately there's been a lot of talk about the "periodization of exercise" for peak performance. Basically, periodization means varying your training program—whatever that may be—at regular time intervals for peak performance.

What's true of performance is also true of your energy deficit. Remember that the body is always looking for that point of adaptation; it really, really, really wants to adjust to whatever you're doing so that it protects its coveted energy stores. That means whatever you do to lose fat, it wants to fight you to keep it. Exercise is no different. If you do the same exercise, with same frequency or the same weight, at the same time, your body will adapt to it, and the benefit will be lost.

To my way of thinking, *any* exercise is good exercise. But why stop at good? If you're going to the trouble to suit up and head to the gym, why not make it pay off by switching things up so that your body doesn't turn a good thing into a bad one?

Code Cracker

When we create an energy deficit, the body must look to fat sooner for an energy source.

Key 4: Produce Heat

The fourth adaptive response to manipulate is the body's needs for constant and continual energy to support all functions. When the body doesn't have a continual source of energy in the form of regular meals, it comes under the assumption the last meal you gave it is the last meal it may get. Your eating pattern determines how and if your body uses the food you take in immediately or tries to store it for later use.

Code Cracker

To counter this adaptive response, we schedule five to six meals throughout your fourteen- to sixteen-hour waking day.

To crack the fat-loss code, we have to become very conscious of when we eat. While it is important to create an energy deficit by reducing calories and/or exercising, this program is *not* about starving yourself. This is a *life*style, not a *diet*!

To keep your body from reacting to a long period of going without food, thus shutting off your body's thermostat (and slowing down your metabolic rate and thyroid function), we instead provide regular intervals of eating five to six meals throughout your day. This way, your body doesn't go into "survival mode" and send a red alert to your hormones to store more fat as a preventive measure.

Eating smaller meals more often, especially meals containing protein, causes an increase in metabolism through the digestive process and a balance of blood sugar levels. To use fat as an energy source, we need to heat up the body, through balancing calorie intake, the digestive process, and the regulation of our thyroid hormones.

Remember, it's not enough just to move fat from storage to the bloodstream; we must then use fat. Now that we can directly grab fat with these five keys, we must somehow act upon that fat to effectively "lose" it.

This can be compared to putting wood on the fire. The more wood you put on the fire, the hotter it burns. The hotter the fire burns, the more wood the fire consumes. The fire's spark can be compared to the internal spark produced by the body's thyroid hormones, which keep your metabolism burning.

> ### Code Cracker
> When we heat up the body, energy is used, and fat becomes a direct source of fuel.

Key 5: Manipulate Energy Stores

A big part of cracking the fat-loss code is actually manipulating energy stores so your body can effectively use all its excess fat and use the food you eat much more efficiently as immediate energy, instead of storing it as fat. Macro-patterning—carefully regulating your PFC (protein, fat, and carbohydrate) intake as well as alternating it—combats the body's adaptive response so that it never knows what hit it.

Macro-patterning allows us to manipulate glycogen levels stored in the muscle and liver to create an energy deficit (key 3) without the body knowing it and responding with the adaptive response. Remember, the minute the body thinks you're on a diet, it moves heaven and earth to go into anti-diet mode, basically doing anything and everything it can to keep as much fat as possible in your body's "energy savings account," because it knows you're going into starvation mode. If the body knows you're on a diet, it will send the rest of the body a signal to conserve energy for the coming dry spell. That means it shuts down body temperature, reduces absorption rate, and slows down your metabolism, all with an eye on storing more fat so it will have plenty of energy, just in case.

When we crack the fat-loss code, we take two days a week to lower glycogen levels just enough for the body to go grab fat, and then we replace it so the body doesn't perceive starvation. It's kind of like sleight of hand; from time to time we have to "trick" the body into thinking it's not losing fat, when actually that's exactly the goal we're trying to achieve.

Code Cracker

When we *crack the fat-loss code,* we take two days a week to lower glycogen levels just enough for the body to go grab fat, and then we replace it so the body doesn't perceive starvation.

Another reason we manipulate glycogen levels up and down on our macro-patterning program is to lower glycogen stores just long enough to get the body to use stored fat for energy. Remember, we want to leave enough in checking (glycogen stored in muscles) for you to meet your daily needs, but we want to force the body to dip into its savings account (energy stored as fat) more often.

The best part about manipulating the body's energy stores is that, ultimately, we can get the body to store less fat altogether, giving you higher sustained energy levels. That's right; when you manipulate glycogen stores over a long period of time, the body takes what it's eating and forces it to be used for sustained energy levels, instead of storage as fat.

The body is stubborn, but it *can* be trained. It wants you to survive; that's why it stores fat. It thinks that by saving up plenty of energy, it can keep you healthy in case of emergency. But that's just your cave dweller brain thinking! Today we don't need to hunt and gather our food, so there is rarely a time when we'll need to save all that fat in case of emergency. Just the opposite is true: our food is too convenient, too readily available. With double- to triple-sized portions being the norm rather

"My Life Has Really Changed for the Better"
Susan Newton

I joined ForeverFit in January of 2007. At that time I really was not in good physical or emotional health. I had an elevated triglyceride level, my cholesterol was near 200, my blood sugar was borderline, my blood pressure was very high, and I was depressed. I did not realize I was depressed until after I had been in the Nutrition Boot Camp for a couple of weeks. Thanks to Wendy for sharing her plan in Cracking the Fat-Loss Code.

I am now forty-five pounds lighter, and my triglycerides are normal, my cholesterol is 178, my blood pressure is down, and I am now off one of my medications, and the other two have been cut in half. Word from my doctors is that I may be able to come off of them altogether very shortly, as my blood pressure is now too low. I feel great and have more energy than I thought possible. I really joined the boot camp to have more energy, as I was very fatigued. No more! I feel great, and my husband is so proud of me—and that means the world to me.

My life has really changed for the better, and I am now healthy and fit. I thought this would be hard, but as Wendy says, "Just do it." I had to remember that when I got a little tempted. Just do it. We did—and I say "we" because Wendy and her team really helped, and she is always there to answer any questions or to help solve any problem I may have. Thank you, Wendy.

than the exception, we are eating too much and storing too much fat.

We need to teach our cave dweller brains the modern way of thinking. We do not need to be walking around with excess baggage, because we can learn for ourselves how best to eat for maximum performance. The payoff is rediscovering the joys of eating again. You remember my friend, business partner, and former boot camper, Rachel, from the Introduction. After losing 107 pounds in her first year on our program, Rachel has managed to keep it off. Now, several years later, she is a shining example of what it can mean to truly discover the joys of eating. Today Rachel is satisfied with less food, more often. Through the science of macro-patterning, she is highly attuned to her body's needs, as well as her senses. Years of excess calories and extra-large portions made her nearly immune to the taste of her food. Now she knows immediately if something's too salty or too sweet. She once told me it was "like her senses came out of hibernation."

Isn't it time your senses came out of hibernation, too?

 FAT-LOSS FACT

A big part of cracking the fat-loss code is actually manipulating the energy stores, or effectively telling the body how much it can store of what, and where.

4

Eight Weeks to Cracking the Code and Breaking Your Plateau

Two Months to a Brand-New You

I f you think about it, two months is so short. Look back on your life, and try to pinpoint a time when two months meant more than the blink of an eye. Can you remember two months from kindergarten? Junior high? College? Well, I'm here to give you an even bigger bang for your buck: give me two months, and I'll give you your life back!

I am not a drill instructor. I am not here to yell at you or blame you or dredge up your past. We've all made mistakes. What's done is done. But today is a new today; this day is about you. Give yourself two months, and get your life back.

Starting things is hard, I know. Starting difficult things, where the risk of failure is great, is even harder. And especially when it comes to dieting, we often feel doomed to fail. That's not just because the human body doesn't respond to dieting, it's because we have all failed at dieting so often. The more we've failed at something in the past, the more likely we are to fail again at it in the future.

Code Cracker

If you'll give me eight weeks, I promise to give you your life back!

One of the "flaws" of the miraculous human body (if we can really call it a flaw) is that the body is so good as a machine that most things we do to it have no immediate effect. The amazing body continues to thrive even when we feed it junk food and move half as much as we should. It's amazing how well our bodies work, considering how badly we treat them!

The consequences of poor eating habits and not enough exercise aren't always immediate. In fact, it takes time for poor eating and exercise habits to really take their toll. So in the grand scheme of things, we continue to put off changing our habits, thinking we will get to it sometime, but unfortunately, "sometime" never gets here.

Now the time is here; this time can be different. Every year, you get fifty-two weeks to change, improve, enhance, live, love, and enjoy your life. I need only eight of them to make the other forty-four spring to life. If you'll give me eight weeks, I promise to give you your life back!

Code Cracker

Starting things is hard, I know. Starting difficult things, where the risk of failure is great, is even harder.

Crack the Fat-Loss Code provides not only an intensive, eight-week process for losing the fat, but also a lifelong maintenance program based on macro-patterning, or regulating how and when you take in protein, fat, and carbohydrates to avoid storing more fat. But this is no rigid system based on denial. The food plans are generous, simple, and easy to tailor to your own needs.

The beauty of these meal plans is that they are not generic. They are personalized for men and women, as well as for people who have diabetes and those who want to lose ten, thirty, or even a hundred pounds or more. Even people who have no weight to lose can learn how macro-patterning can improve their energy levels and long-term health. The plan even allows for alterations if you reach your goal in less than eight weeks. Everyone can work with our plan to lose fat and break through his or her dieting plateau forever.

There is a reason your program lasts eight weeks and not eight days (or eight months). For all your life, the body has been the teacher and you its student. Now it's time to turn the tables. In the next eight weeks, you will be teaching your body where to go for energy. Most of the time, your body tells you what it needs; these signals are called "cravings," and they're the reason why you drink when you're thirsty and eat when you're hungry.

Your body is so good, it can even tell you what kinds of foods you need more of and even less of. Have you ever looked at that last slice of pizza in the fridge after finishing off the other seven slices all week and thought to yourself, "I can't eat another slice"? That's your body telling you that you need something fresh.

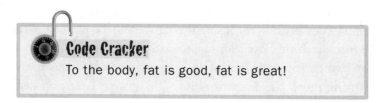

Code Cracker

To the body, fat is good, fat is great!

Unfortunately, your body cares more about its physical needs than about your emotions. Your body doesn't care if being a little fat has thrown you into a deep depression or made you feel isolated and insecure. To the body, fat is good, fat is great! And, partially, it's right; you need a certain amount of fat in your diet and on your body.

But now it's time for you to treat fat differently. For too long, the body has been keeping around lots and lots of fat as its "last resort" for energy. It's there; your body's just not using it. No longer—over the next eight weeks, you will teach the body to "go get fat" and use it first, not last. You will be the teacher, and the body will be your student.

Understanding the Four Cycles of the Fat-Loss Code

Your eight-week fat-loss program is divided into four cycles. These cycles are the key to cracking the fat-loss code. You've been given the reasons, the facts—the "why," if you will. Now I'm giving you the "how."

Cycle 1: Carb-Deplete Cycle

Deplete is a serious word for serious business, but that's exactly what you're going to be doing in the first week of your program. I call it your seven-day diet. And that's the only time I use the word *diet* to refer to my program, and I use it in the strictest sense of the term. This is when you're restricting certain foods (particularly carbs) and manipulating the amount of glycogen that is stored in the muscle. During the Carb-Deplete Cycle, you are going to shut off the body's dependence upon sugar and teach it where fat stores are available for energy needs.

Cycle 2: Macro-Patterning Cycle

After the first week of your program, you will begin your Macro-Patterning Cycle. This is where you begin to pattern the body for fat loss and slow its adaptive response. This cycle includes three kinds of days:

1. **Baseline days:** As the name implies, we want to give your body a baseline to start from. This baseline will be drastically different from what your body is used to; this is what we want. The trick is not to find the body's point of adaptation and stay there, but to force the body to adapt—and then keep adapting. To that end, these days will consist of basic nutrient intake containing proteins through the day and one starch with two different meals before 3:00 P.M. Any fat intake will be from mostly "good fat" sources.

2. **Carb-down days:** Now it's time to rely on our good friends the carbs to help you teach the body how to burn fat efficiently. To help your body reduce its dependency on glycogen stores in the muscle for energy use, we are going to continue to regulate just how much glycogen—or energy derived from carbs—is stored in the muscle. To that end, on these days, you will have minimal carb intake to force the body to use fat as an energy source. Protein is still required through the day. In these days, you'll have one starch with a protein meal before 3:00 P.M. and fat intake from only "good fat" sources.

3. **Carb-up days (Food Passes):** During carb-up days, you will use an increased amount of starches to spark your body's metabolic rate and provide the body with nutrients for repair and growth. On these days, the last two meals contain primarily carbohydrates. There are two carb-up days a week, and they

immediately follow a carb-down day. My clients affectionately call carb-up days their Food Passes—two days a week when you can let loose, splurge a little, and enjoy foods typically forbidden on other plans, like bread, desserts, pizza, and even alcohol.

Typically, carb-up days are Wednesdays and Saturdays, so you can go out Saturday night with your friends and enjoy yourself. As an added benefit, you determine which two days are your carb-up days for the week, so you can plan ahead. Because holidays, birthdays, and other special occasions don't always fall on a Wednesday or a Saturday, the Food Passes are very convenient and extremely interchangeable.

Code Cracker

The best part about the Food Passes is that you can plan around them and use them as the need arises.

Cycle 3: Accelerated Fat-Loss Cycle

Although I rely largely on manipulating carbohydrates to help you teach the body how to use excess fat stores as energy, this is not a high- or low-carb diet. (Actually, it's not a diet at all.) This is about fat loss. So for our third cycle, we want to pick up the pace a little and engage in the Accelerated Fat-Loss Cycle. Don't worry if it seems familiar; these are basically the same types of days found in the Macro-Patterning Cycle, with changes in how they are cycled to provide an increase in the usage of fat stores.

Cycle 4: Maintenance Cycle

You can't be on a continuous diet. Living ForeverFit is a long-term lifestyle, and living on a lifelong diet is not the answer to enjoying life and living well. During the first three cycles, you've been sprinting—running to catch up and teach your body about using fat for energy. But you can't sprint forever.

The fourth cycle, the Maintenance Cycle, is also used for vacations and to aid in setting a new weight set point for the body to learn to maintain. This is the time that the body resets itself back to a higher nutrient profile in favor of carbohydrates and fats. During the Maintenance Cycle, you will learn how to live forever fit. The beauty of the Maintenance Cycle is that it can last forever.

We add two days to the Maintenance Cycle:

1. **Cheat day:** During the Maintenance Cycle, you can have foods not normally on the plan, any food you like. This includes carbs, alcohol, etc. (Just don't stuff.)

2. **High-carb day:** During high-carb days, you're having carbs through your day. Of course you're still learning, and maintaining, so make sure they are "clean" starches, not sugary ones like doughnuts and cakes.

FAT-LOSS FACT

This is about fat loss. We're all about cracking the fat-loss code, remember?

How to Put the Four Cycles in Motion

Welcome to the rest of your life! That's right: on the following pages you will begin to understand the four cycles better. I know it may take some getting used to. All these letters, P and S and V and SA, all these symbols, CH and B, C and D, can look daunting at first. But in this section, I'll lay each one out for you and tell you exactly what they all mean.

For starters, you will find that each type of food has a key:

- **P** is for protein.
- **S** is for starch.
- **V** is for vegetable.
- **O** is for fat.
- **A** is for fruit.
- **SA** is for sweets and alcohol.

Each week starts with its own set of rules; follow these closely! While this is not a diet, the closer you stay to the guidelines described in each week, the better your results will be. These weeks and the cycles they fall within are designed specifically to alter the body's adaptive process. So read through the rules carefully, and I promise you'll find they're very easy to follow.

After the rules, you'll find a helpful weekly planner that shows you exactly how each day of the week shapes up.

As you begin to study your meal plans more closely, you will be reminded of the types of days you'll find during this part of your plan:

- **A** stands for deplete day.
- **B** stands for baseline day.
- **C** stands for carb-down day.
- **D** stands for carb-up day.
- **CH** stands for cheat day.
- **H** stands for high-carb day.

"A Family Affair"

Jim Myers

We started Nutrition Boot Camp after hearing about the program through a friend. By far, this diet is the best program we have ever tried. Trust me, my family and I have tried them all. (We're owners of an Italian restaurant, so much of our life is centered around food—weight has always been an issue.) I started the eight-week program along with my wife, mother-in-law, and brother-in-law. After the initial eight-week program, the four of us lost a combined total of approximately one hundred pounds, and we started the plan just before Thanksgiving! I personally lost twenty pounds during this period.

I have been on the program with Wendy for approximately eight months. During that time, I have lost a total of thirty pounds. What's more important to me is that my cholesterol numbers have improved dramatically. Just after the initial eight weeks, my total cholesterol count went from 265 to 155, and my triglycerides went from 495 to 172. There are many reasons to enjoy this diet. The best thing I like about it is the fact that you are not hungry all day long. You eat several meals per day! The next best thing would be that my energy level has improved dramatically. Instead of being sluggish throughout the day, I truly feel energized and sleep more soundly during the night.

We all highly recommend this diet plan to anyone who wants to lose weight and/or simply wants to improve his or her health. Many diets out there starve the body of the nutrients it needs. Not only does Wendy's plan help you learn the right things to eat, but it also combines the nutrition plan with simple exercise techniques that, when combined, work like magic.

It may look funny to you now, but by weeks 2 and 3, you'll be familiar with B, C, D, and A, and you'll know how to structure your meal plans accordingly. The beauty of the system is how flexible it is. Within each specific day, you'll find a full substitution list of all the various foods you can have. I think you'll be pleasantly surprised by just how many of your favorite foods are on these lists and how much of them you can have. Truly, the combinations are endless!

And as if the substitution lists weren't enough, I provide some of my favorite recipes for each cycle. Best of all, these are fresh, delicious, quick, and easy dishes to prepare, from my favorite Wendy's Egg Cheeseburger to Grilled Shrimp Kebabs to Wendy's Crepes to my Mocha Protein Shake. I guarantee you'll love these recipes as much as my clients do.

Also, in Chapter 10, I provide a complete week of sample meal plans for each of the four cycles explained in the previous pages. As an added bonus, Chapter 12 gives recipes for more variation and fresh meal choices. You can enjoy them as you read along and then get the bonus experience of new sample meal plans and recipes collected in two convenient chapters for when your reading's done.

I am truly excited that you've made the decision to crack the fat-loss code, and I hope this mini road map provides you with the same enthusiasm for the journey you're about to undertake.

5

Cycle 1

Carb-Deplete Cycle, Week 1

Welcome to week 1 of your eight-week program, otherwise known as the Carb-Deplete Cycle or, as we refer to it in Nutrition Boot Camp, your "seven-day diet." That's because this is the one week—really, the only week—where we're all about leaving foods out, forbidding foods. The rest of your program is all about adding back; the first week is all about leaving out.

Why do we do this? Recall that glycogen is stored in the muscle. If glycogen is there, the body will use glycogen instead of fat for energy. It's just that simple; we are trying to redirect where your body goes to find fat. So for the first seven days of your program, you're going to reduce, or cut off, your carbohydrates so that you can lower glycogen stores and deplete how much glycogen is stored in the muscle. This way you can teach your body to "go get fat" instead of glycogen.

Depleting glycogen stores can't be achieved overnight. So that no new glycogen is stored in the muscle as energy, you restrict the intake of carbohydrates, your body's quickest, easiest source of quick energy and the main contributor of glycogen stores in the body.

It takes a full seventy-two hours—three straight days—to deplete the body of glycogen. We do it so that if no glycogen is present, the body will learn to go get fat. Fat will be its only source of energy. Now the body has a reason to go find fat. This is a valuable lesson that, once learned, makes it easier for the body to crack the fat-loss code and begin looking elsewhere for energy.

FAT-LOSS FACT

It takes a full seventy-two hours—three straight days—to deplete the body of glycogen.

For this reason, you must follow your food plan very, very carefully during the first seven days. It wasn't generated by accident or quickly; your food plan, and the meal guides for each day, were carefully calculated so that you would eat less than 20 grams of carbohydrates per day during this Carb-Deplete Cycle.

Fortunately, I've taken all the guesswork out of how to eat, what to eat, and when. The meal plans here and in Chapter 10 include a complete menu of daily meals for men, women, and people with diabetes. Here you will find a complete sampling of times of day, meals and portion sizes, mini recipes, and complete substitution lists, so you have choices, not restriction. Even during the first seven days of your plan, I want you to have variety and choice. However, you must remember that this is the most rigid and "forbidden" time of your program; be precise in what you eat and how much. Follow the plan precisely, and this week will be much easier for you.

This first week is all about teaching and retraining your body to find energy elsewhere. Depleting your glycogen stores will take time and effort. The better you do during these seven days, the easier the rest of the program—and your eventual fat loss—will be.

Remember, too, that these foods are all easy to find in your local grocery store or health food store, but you don't even need a health food store. These are no special foods; you're not buying them from me, so you won't find any prepackaged "fake foods."

Proteins include eggs, protein shakes, cottage cheese, fresh fish, lean beef, tuna packed in water, turkey, and chicken breast. During the Carb-Deplete Cycle, you will be eating protein at each meal.

Vegetables are a vital part of any food program, and mine is no different. You will see in your meal plan that you are to eat only certain vegetables during the first seven days; after the first seven days, no vegetable is forbidden (with a few exceptions). As you consult your substitution list, notice that the number next to each vegetable represents the number of active carbs per cup. (See the full list following the meal plans in this chapter.)

Code Cracker

Count carbs; carbs count! Remember, you must be at 20 grams or less during this first seven days.

Your fat requirements during the first seven days of your program will vary from what you'll find during the other seven weeks. Since you are drastically reducing your carbohydrate intake, your body will need to find an energy-rich, calorie-dense food source somewhere. Fat is your answer. In fact, fat is a way to sustain you during this first week on your plan.

Count carbs; carbs count! Remember, you must be at 20 grams or less during this first seven days. Being exact on the plan makes you a good teacher. Playing loose and fast with the rules only sends your body mixed messages. Your body can, and will, learn to go elsewhere to find energy, but only if you teach it properly.

Remember that we are entering a phase—and a lifestyle— where we treat our body logically, not emotionally. Logic implies reason, and the reasonable way to approach the first seven days of your program is to be precise. There is not as much wiggle room during this week as there will be on the rest of the program.

After the first seven days, there is room for error; during the first seven days, there really is no room for error.

I like to tell the story of Chrissy, a young woman in my class who took three weeks to get through her first seven days! Why? Simple: she had blueberry pancakes in the middle of the night, every night. I would tell Chrissy, "Blueberry pancakes aren't a 'quick grab' meal in the middle of the night. We're talking full-out cooking here. That cheat took a lot of planning: making batter, heating a skillet, plating and eating it."

She would say it just was a habit she had been doing forever. She wouldn't eat until lunch and tried not to eat much dinner. She was literally starving herself, and then she couldn't sleep until she had something sweet. Then she started the whole cycle over again, day after day. Folks, that's gonna stop you every time!

You have to work at this a little, have some easy-grab stuff prepared, like salads and turkey breast rolled with cheese and some veggies. Follow the food plans, and don't be like Chrissy, my "blueberry pancake" lady, who took three weeks to complete her first seven days.

During this first week, look for the "shift." One of the things you'll notice after three or four days is that you'll have a clear time when your energy shifts down, and then you'll experience high energy and a sense of well-being. This is the shift.

The shift is the positive part of high energy that comes from the body finding fat. Because the body runs with higher energy when using fat, this shift can feel unfamiliar (yet great) because we're so used to never even going near fat for energy. It's a new experience—and a fun one! As your program goes along, you'll feel the shift less strongly, because more and more hours of more and more days will be spent with this sense of high energy and well-being.

In essence, you've shifted gears—and you'll stay there.

FAT-LOSS FACT

This first week is all about teaching your body to find energy elsewhere. Depleting your glycogen stores takes time and effort.

Rules for the Carb-Deplete Cycle

The success of your entire plan depends very much upon the first seven days. Be precise, logical, and rational. These rules must be followed *exactly*. It is very important during this week that you count *any and all* carbohydrates you take in. Remember, your carbohydrate total must be *under 20 grams*. Follow the plan exactly, and, should you make any substitutions, make sure to *count the carbs*.

• **Be exact.** Write down everything that goes in your mouth, so you know what and how many carbs you consumed that day.

• **Keep track of what you're taking in every day.** Use the log sheets found in Chapter 11, or order the ForeverFit log book from our website to keep track, because that way, you can see what you're eating and doing.

• **Timing matters.** Eat every three to four hours up until two hours before bed. Think of your body as a car. The tank on your car holds only so much gas; when it says "E," you have to go get gas. Your body works the same way. It holds only enough fuel for three to four hours of energy at one time. People with diabetes need to make sure they eat protein before bed and immediately upon rising; they have been "fasting" all night.

• **Get your daily minimum.** I prefer you eat five small meals, but you must have a minimum of four meals each day. In the sample food plans in this chapter and Chapter 10, there are examples of six meals. Don't force meals, but do eat at least four.

• **Control your portions.** Limit portion size to the size of your fist. (When eating out, ask for a to-go container at the beginning of your meal, and portion-control your food.) Portions have gotten out of hand. Restaurants are trying to provide more food for less money, so you're often getting two meals in one. If you're like me, you were taught as a child to eat everything on your plate. The guilt sets in if you don't clean your plate. Learn new rules; set aside half your meal in your to-go container, and eat what's left on your plate. This simple tip has many benefits: not only do you save another meal for later, but you have no guilt about going out for dinner, and most importantly, you avoid overeating.

• **Monitor your carb intake.** Carbohydrate intake *must be under 20 grams* of "active carbs" per day. Carbs minus fiber equals active carbs. Check your food label. To get the active carbs, subtract the amount of fiber from the carbohydrate total.

• **Drink your minimum amount of water each day.** For women, the minimum is 70 to 80 ounces; for men, it's 100 to 128 ounces per day. In the absence of water, your body stores carbohydrates for its hydration needs, so if you're a poor water drinker, you would literally be shutting off your body's water supply via reduced carbs. That means you must add extra water, not less. If you're feeling fatigued during this week, it's OK to add (a little) fat from your substitution list. This week is about depleting carbs, not fat. Add oils to your salads. This will give you energy and the needed calories for energy.

- **Stay away from fruit and fruit juice.** After seven days, there are no forbidden foods or juices, but for now, don't have any fruit or fruit juice.

- **Beware of sauces and toppings, as they may have hidden carbs.** Even ketchups and condiments might have carbs. Be careful about hidden carbs, so the seven-day plan can work. You can go over your limit and not even know it if you don't read labels or if you order saucy foods in restaurants.

- **Eat foods on the meal planner or substitution lists.** If you want foods that aren't on the meal planner for this week, stick to choices from the substitution lists for the Carb-Deplete Cycle. Closely follow your lists during this week.

- **Make sure to have one serving of broccoli per day.** Broccoli and the other vegetables listed during this week are thermic; they produce heat. Broccoli also has a lot of fiber, which is something you need during your first week because of all the extra proteins and fats you may not be used to during this week. Constipation can be a problem, so make sure to eat 1 cup of broccoli each day.

- **Avoid protein bars and "low-carb" foods.** These bars and their low-carb counterparts contain so many chemicals and additives, to the point where these foods are unsafe. Instead, eat whole foods, good foods, *real* foods. If it doesn't taste natural, it's most likely not.

- **Skip the alcohol.** Not this week; sorry. Later, and soon, alcohol will shift back onto your food plan, but for now, abstaining from alcohol is a must.

- **Don't force meals or eat too much at each meal.** A good rule of thumb is that if you get to your next meal and aren't hungry, you ate too much at your previous meal. If you are starving before it's time to eat again, then you didn't eat enough at your previous meal.

• **Positive attitude counts.** Surround yourself with positive people, and seek the support of others. These are the people who are close to you and want to see you succeed. Our website (see More About ForeverFit Programs and Services following the appendixes) offers support through our member area and forums, and we're always just a phone call or e-mail away.

Weekly Meal Plan for the Carb-Deplete Cycle

Here you will find your weekly meal plan for the Carb-Deplete Cycle:

Week 1 Meal Plan

Planner A	Mon Day 1	Tues Day 2	Wed Day 3	Thurs Day 4	Fri Day 5	Sat Day 6	Sun Day 7
Carb- Deplete Cycle	Carbs: Under 20 g	Carbs: Under 20 g	Carbs: Under 20 g	Carbs: Under 20 g	Carbs: Under 20 g	Carbs: Under 20 g	Carbs: Under 20 g

Substitution Food Lists for the Carb-Deplete Cycle

Use these lists as a way to substitute foods on your sample meal planner based on the type of food for each meal required. When substituting, you must consume the appropriate portion size.

Type P = Protein Requirements and Substitutions
• Consume protein at each meal, at least four times per day. Five meals are ideal.

- Consume the amount of protein listed on the meal planner. An estimate is OK, but weighing your food after it is cooked is best. Remember, protein amounts are given for cooked weight. When you order out, restaurants list the weight precooked on the menu, but meat cooks down by 1 or 2 ounces.
- Cottage cheese may be consumed only once per day.
- If you are consuming a protein shake, use a shake with less than 1 gram of sugar or less and carbs under 6 grams. Adjust the serving for not more than 25 grams (approximately 3 to 4 ounces) of protein for women and 40 grams (approximately 5 to 8 ounces) for men.
- When eating egg whites, you may have one whole egg with your whites if desired.
- Eat any of the following proteins. You need to count carbohydrates only where indicated:
  - Egg whites or egg substitute
  - Protein shake (**count carbs**)
  - Cottage cheese (**count carbs**)
  - Fresh fish: salmon, trout, etc.
  - Lean beef
  - Tuna, canned in water
  - Turkey breast
  - Chicken breast

Type V = Vegetable Requirements and Substitutions

- Consume *only* the following vegetables during your Carb-Deplete Cycle. The carbohydrate amounts per cup are listed next to each. Labels that you read for these may not correspond to the number we have listed next to these veggies. We identify the number by the way these veggies affect the body, not by their nutrient content. Use our number.
  - Asparagus (2 grams of carbs per cup)
  - Broccoli (4 grams per cup)
  - Cabbage (1 gram per cup)

- Celery (0 grams per cup)
- Cucumber (0 grams per cup)
- Lettuce (0 grams per cup)
- Mushrooms (1 gram per cup)
- Radicchio (0 grams per cup)
- Radishes (0 grams per cup)
- Spinach (1 gram per cup)
- You can have vegetables at any meal as long as you don't go over 20 grams of carbs for that day, and as long as you eat them with a protein. There is no need to eat between meals and graze like cattle, as long as you're eating the appropriate portion.

Type O = Fat Requirements and Substitutions

- Have only one serving of fat at each meal. To find the serving size, use the nutrition facts label on the package.
  - Mayonnaise
  - Flaxseed oil
  - Olive oil
  - Cheese
  - Butter

Condiments

- You may use any condiments, but remember to check carb counts. Don't buy or consume processed "no-carb" or "low-carb" condiments, sauces, or dressings.

Code Cracker

Consume protein at each meal, four times minimum per day, five meals ideal.

Sample Daily Meal Plan for the Carb-Deplete Cycle

Here you will find your sample daily meal plan for the Carb-Deplete Cycle:

Carb-Deplete Cycle Meal Plan A: Sample Carb-Deplete Day

MEAL	TYPE	WOMEN	MEN
1	P/O	**Wendy's Egg Cheeseburger** (See page 87.)	**Wendy's Egg Cheeseburger** (See page 87.)
2	P/O	½ cup cottage cheese (full-fat brand so carbs are reduced)	1 cup cottage cheese (full-fat brand so carbs are reduced)
3	P/V/O	Chicken Caesar salad: 3–4 oz. chicken on large lettuce and cucumber salad with 1 tbsp. extra-virgin olive oil and vinegar (watch carb count)	Chicken Caesar salad: 3–4 oz. chicken on large lettuce and cucumber salad with 1 tbsp. extra-virgin olive oil and vinegar (watch carb count)
4	P/O	**Orange Dream Protein Shake** (See page 89.)	**Orange Dream Protein Shake** (See page 89.)
5	P/V/O	4–6 oz. broiled salmon or halibut 1 cup broccoli Lettuce and cucumber salad with 1 tbsp. extra-virgin olive oil and vinegar or full-fat dressing (watch carb count)	6–8 oz. broiled salmon or halibut 1 cup broccoli Lettuce and cucumber salad with 1 tbsp. extra-virgin olive oil and vinegar or full-fat dressing (watch carb count)
6	P/O	**Mocha Protein Shake** (See page 90.)	**Mocha Protein Shake** (See page 90.)
Type Key			
P = Protein V = Vegetable O = Fat			

Notes

1. This sample food plan shows six meals. If you consume only four meals, you may skip meal 2 or 4 and meal 6, for a total of four meals that day.

2. If you consume only five meals, then you may skip meal 2 or 4 or 6, for a total of five meals.

3. If you would like to substitute a different food at any particular meal, you must follow the type listed next to that meal and substitute the same type of food from your substitution list.

Your Notes

_____

_____

_____

_____

_____

_____

_____

_____

_____

_____

_____

_____

_____

Wendy's Top-Ten Carb-Deplete Shopping List Items

When it comes to making changes to your daily eating habits, the first week on your plan will be a challenge. The good news is that, now more than ever before, it is easier to make smart choices at restaurants and at your local grocery store. Restaurants now see substituting menu choices as mainstream, rather than "special orders."

Grocery stores are continually making improvements and now have larger sections than ever before of organic produce, meats, and packaged goods. Food is also packaged conveniently. A great example is prewashed and bagged lettuce—what a time saver that is. Another of my favorites is broccoli florets cut, washed, and bagged. You no longer have to chop down the whole spears.

With all this convenience and ease, I have developed my own way of prepping food and adding flavors to foods with seasonings instead of sauces. For those of you who enjoy cooking with recipes, take heart. After the first week (and the occasional carb-down day), there is literally no food forbidden, so feel free to pull out any of your family's favorites.

Following each section of meal planners in this book, I have compiled a few of my clients' and my own personal favorite recipes, along with additional recipes in Chapter 12.

Here are a few tips that I have found make meal shopping, planning, and prepping easier. *Enjoy!*

Code Cracker

The good news is that, now more than ever before, it is easier to make smart choices at restaurants and at your local grocery store.

"I Lost Seven Pounds That First Week"
Debbie Cummings

As I turn forty-five years old today, I am truly amazed when I look back at where I was a year ago before I found this program. When I had moved to Florida a couple of years ago, I thought that I would get healthy and lead this very active lifestyle. Instead, I gained twenty pounds and was eating every sweet and junky food that I could get in my mouth. I was miserable; none of my clothes fit, but I refused to go shopping to buy larger clothes. I had horrible digestive issues that made me feel even more bloated and uncomfortable.

I had tried many different diet plans in the past, and while I lost a few pounds in the beginning, I never really achieved my goals, nor was I able to keep off the weight that I'd lost. A coworker had been going to Nutrition Boot Camp for several months, experienced substantial weight loss, and looked great. So, on June 22, 2006, I decided to give it a try—it was a day that changed my life forever. I was really nervous when I read what I had to do the first week, but I was still determined to make it work. Not only did I make it through that week, I lost seven pounds. I was hooked!

I have since lost all that weight and have gained tone and definition I never thought possible, especially at my age. This time last year, I struggled to get through thirty minutes on the treadmill, and weight training wasn't even on my radar. I can now knock out three miles in that same thirty minutes and lift weights three or four times per week. Following the program and exercising have become a part of who I am. I know that if I have a bad day or even a few bad days, Wendy has taught me how to get back on track and not go back to where I was before. I am a size 6, a size I have never been in my life! This is pretty amazing, especially considering I was pushing a size 12 a year ago. My previous digestive issues no longer bother me.

Wendy and Rachel have been my support and inspiration. I highly recommend this program to anyone who is looking to lose and keep off the weight, and who is looking to improve their self-confidence and self-image. The program is not a diet; it's not an exercise routine; it's a lifestyle. And it works.

Shopping can be intimidating for most of us, especially when starting any new lifestyle or creating new habits. My Top-Ten Carb-Deplete Shopping List Items should take the fear out of your next trip to the grocery store:

1. **Liquid egg whites:** Without a doubt, packaged egg whites are something you will always find in my refrigerator. Remember, eggs are the best protein source you can consume. This convenient packaging makes life easy when cooking.

2. **Turkey breast luncheon meat:** Buy the lower-sodium, no-MSG version. When you have it sliced at the deli, ask the staff put a piece of paper wrap between each 3- to 4-ounce portion so it is already weighed for you.

3. **Precut broccoli florets:** For perfectly steamed broccoli, take a double sheet of paper towel, place it on a plate, and on one side pile your fresh broccoli. Cover up the broccoli with the other side, and fold it under so it is wrapped tight. Sprinkle some water on the top (don't soak it, but wet it some). Place the plate in the microwave, and cook on high for about 3 minutes. You will have to experiment, as microwaves vary, and the cooking time also depends on how you like your broccoli. I like mine very tender, not too crunchy.

4. **Prewashed and bagged lettuce:** The first week, this is really a big help, since lettuce carries a zero carb count.

5. **Cucumber:** I always have a cucumber already cut up in a container in the fridge, so it is easy to grab to put in a salad. When eating out during the Carb-Deplete Cycle, I have never been to a restaurant that wouldn't make a lettuce and cucumber salad. Just ask!

|||||||||||||| **FAT-LOSS FACT** ||||||||||||||
Remember, eggs are the best protein source you can consume.

6. **Boneless, skinless chicken breast:** This is a great, versatile, low-calorie source of protein. I buy all my meat antibiotic- and hormone-free, and most grocery stores carry many different brands without you having to shop at specialty food markets. Let me tell you the secret to making perfect moist chicken every time. First, when grilling any chicken or any meat, grill on high heat. I have found that most chicken breasts take only 5 to 6 minutes on both sides on the grill. Here is the secret part: after 5 to 6 minutes of cooking time, remove the chicken from the grill, and put it in a glass container with a glass lid, *not* plastic. Let it sit on the counter for about 20 minutes. The chicken will continue to cook and redistribute its juices while steaming in the glass. Most people try to cook their chicken totally done on the grill, and because the chicken will continue to cook when removed from the grill, it ends up dry and overcooked by the time you eat it.

7. **Tuna:** Canned in water or in the new vacuum-packed pouches, tuna is one of the quickest quality protein sources available. It makes a great quick lunchtime meal over a bed of lettuce.

8. **Apple cider vinegar:** This is a great-tasting fat-burning vinegar that you can use without limits during the Carb-Deplete Cycle. Put a couple of "glugs" over a salad with a packet or two of sugar substitute like Splenda, and you have my favorite salad dressing. Not only does it taste fantastic, but it also burns fat because of the cider vinegar's changes in our digestive and enzyme profiles. You also can use it as a marinade for chicken or fish. Pour some in a zip-top plastic bag about one-eighth of the way up the bag. Add a couple of packets of sugar substitute and some dry or fresh rosemary. Or if you like it spicy, add Cajun red pepper. Mmm, good!

9. **Protein shake:** Using a protein shake just makes life easier, especially for travelers, people who keep busy schedules, or people who are just not used to eating so often. I also find that chocolate protein shakes help "chocoholics" overcome that nighttime chocolate fix. There are a lot of different protein

shakes available in the marketplace, and it is trickier than just looking at the label for calories, protein, carbs, and fat. First off, do not choose a shake that is soy based; find one that is whey, milk, or egg based. Make sure that the protein amount is appropriate for your needs. Ladies, you only need a shake that has 20 to 25 grams of protein per serving; in most cases that is 1 scoop. Men really only need 35 to 40 grams, so 1½ scoops would be just right for you. The carbs should be less than 6 grams, and sugar 1 gram or less.

10. **Sugar substitute:** You need to drink plenty of water, especially the first week on your plan, but you don't have to quit drinking coffee or tea if you enjoy those beverages. However, if you want to sweeten it, you will need a sugar substitute. There are several choices on the market. If you want to choose the most natural source, that would be Stevia, a plant-derived sweetener available in packets like other sugar substitutes. I use Splenda substitute in limited quantities. I don't drink diet or regular soda. Instead, I use sugar substitute for my salad dressing, in my coffee or tea, or on my oatmeal. Regular sugar is not allowed during the Carb-Deplete Cycle.

Wendy's "Mmm Good" Favorite Recipes for the Carb-Deplete Cycle

I'm so proud to share with you some of my favorite Carb-Deplete Cycle recipes. These recipes have been tested by my most successful clients—and enjoyed by all of my many boot campers over the years. Better still, they're my favorites as well. Enjoy!

Wendy's Egg Cheeseburger

Use planners A, B, C, D (Planner A is for the Carb-Deplete Cycle.)

> 1 whole egg plus 3 egg whites (women may have only egg whites or egg substitute if desired), or 1 whole egg plus 5 egg whites (men may use egg substitute)
>
> 1½ ounces (for women) or 3 ounces (for men) lean ground beef, cooked and seasoned to taste
>
> A light sprinkle of your favorite cheese, if desired

Spray a nonstick skillet with nonstick cooking spray; place over medium heat. Combine the egg and beef in a bowl. When skillet is hot, pour egg and beef mixture into skillet and cook. When cooked through, remove from skillet, and add a dash of cheese to top.

1 serving

Nutritional Value
Protein: 25 grams / 45 grams
Fat: 7 grams / 12 grams
Carbs: 1 gram

Mushroom and Spinach Omelet

Use planners A, B, C, D (Planner A is for the Carb-Deplete Cycle.)

½ cup sliced mushrooms

1 whole egg plus 3 egg whites (women may have only egg whites or egg substitute if desired), or 1 whole egg plus 5 egg whites (men may use egg substitute, enough to equal 5 egg whites)

Handful fresh spinach or ¼ of small package frozen

A light sprinkle of your favorite cheese, if desired

Spray a nonstick skillet with nonstick cooking spray; place over medium heat. Sauté mushrooms until tender. Beat eggs and combine with spinach. Pour into skillet over mushrooms, and let set. Flip once, and cook until done. When ready, remove from skillet, and sprinkle with cheese if desired.

1 serving

Nutritional Value
Protein: 17 grams / 25 grams
Fat: 3 grams
Carbs: 3 grams

Orange Dream Protein Shake

Use planners A, B, C, D

> 8 to 10 ounces orange-pineapple Crystal Light drink
>
> 4 to 10 ice cubes (fewer for thinner consistency,
>   more for thicker shake)
>
> 1 to 1½ scoops vanilla protein powder (or use the
>   appropriate amount needed)

Pour already prepared Crystal Light drink in blender. Add desired amount of ice. Add protein powder, and blend until smooth. Drink immediately, or put in freezer to thicken.

1 serving

Nutritional Value
Varies according to the kind
    of protein powder used;
    check label for values

Mocha Protein Shake

Use planners A, B, C, D

> 8 to 10 ounces water
>
> 4 to 10 ice cubes (fewer for thinner consistency,
>   more for thicker shake)
>
> 1 heaping teaspoon instant coffee (caffeinated or
>   decaf)
>
> 1 to 1½ scoops chocolate protein powder (or use
>   the appropriate amount needed)

Pour water in the blender. Add coffee and desired amount of ice. Add protein powder, and blend until smooth. Drink immediately, or put in freezer to thicken.

1 serving

Nutritional Value
Varies according to the kind
    of protein powder used;
    check label for values

Turkey and Cheese Lettuce Wrap

Use planners A, B, C, D

> 1 large leaf Bibb lettuce or wide-leaf lettuce
>
> 3 to 4 ounces low-sodium turkey breast luncheon meat
>
> 1 to 2 slices cheese, any kind
>
> 1 tablespoon Smart Balance mayonnaise or deli mustard

Open lettuce leaf flat. Layer with a few slices of turkey, then a slice of cheese, then the rest of the turkey, and then the last slice of cheese. Spread mayo or mustard on top, and roll up tight. Slice in half on an angle, and hold together with a toothpick until you're ready to eat.

1 serving

Nutritional Value
Protein: 25 grams
Fats: 3 grams (depends on
    amount of cheese and
    whether mayo is used)
Carbs: 1 gram

6

Cycle 2

Macro-Patterning Cycle, Weeks 2–4

The first week, the Carb-Deplete Cycle, had a rhyme and reason, and so do the next three weeks. During this critical cycle, we're going to begin to macro-pattern and bring back foods you love and enjoy. The first week of the program was designed to empty out your glycogen stores. We've trained your body to look for energy elsewhere, but we can't stay in that state of emptiness indefinitely. The body seeks balance, and we must abide by certain rules so that the body stays in balance. Emptiness or fullness is not balance; only balance is balance.

We need to reintroduce carbohydrates in a sensible, productive way. Remember that carbohydrates are not the bad guy. This is not a low-carb diet. Only during the first seven days was it important to be so strict and reduce carb intake so severely, simply to begin the process of "cracking the code" and getting your body to understand that there are places to look for energy other than simply utilizing carbohydrates.

During week 2, we begin refilling your body with glycogen, the energy your body stores from the intake of carbohydrates. So week 2 is all about teaching your body to begin regulating glycogen levels. Manipulation into a low state will ensure that fat now can be used as a source of energy.

Think of how you do your weekly shopping, but think of the grocery store as the fat store. Just as you don't go to the grocery store every day, your body doesn't go grab fat that way. Remember, your body wants to hold onto fat, so it won't tap into it daily. Your body relies on glycogen for its regular energy source, so when we lower glycogen, your body will then use fat. So we will ask your body to go shopping twice a week: once in the middle of the week and once at the end of the week. The body doesn't mind going to the fat store if it doesn't feel like it has to go there every day.

This program is all about manipulation of energy through macronutrient intake. We want to take the body out of survival mode and force it to stop reserving and conserving energy for survival, so it will use the food you take in and the excess on the body instead. It is through this process that a better body, better health, and a better life await.

We want to make fat more attractive to the body when it needs energy. The only way to do that is to manipulate the body's glycogen stores. The only way to manipulate the body's glycogen stores is through macro-patterning, or regulating the time and total of protein, carbohydrate, and fat consumption.

Think of your car again. When you're on "E," you know that the tank isn't totally empty. You're not going to run out of gas immediately. You know from experience that you have some wiggle room to go find more gas before you're totally empty. Consider it your car's grace period, if you will.

Code Cracker

Macro-patterning is manipulating glycogen stores through regulating portion amount and timing of protein, carbohydrate, and fat consumption.

The body has a grace period, too. When glycogen stores get low, the body wants to conserve the small amount it has, "just in case." So to avoid bringing those stores down to zero again, you have taught it to go find fat. The more often the body learns to go find fat, the easier and easier it gets to crack the code.

Macro-patterning is teaching your body that it's going to need more and more grace periods when glycogen stores get low. When you learn to crack the fat-loss code, your glycogen stores are always in a state of flux. We can't deplete you totally again; that was more of a kick start to the program, a warning sign and a crash course in finding fat for energy rather than energy stored from carbohydrates.

But we can manipulate those glycogen stores so they are not so readily available—so full all the time—that your body gets back into the habit of using glycogen as its default setting, if you will, for energy use.

Like a car, your body gets full and empty. Like a gas tank, your body's glycogen tanks can get closer to "E" than they have in the past. Weeks 2–4 are all about macro-patterning and manipulating those glycogen stores by carbing up, then carbing down.

As you begin to study your meal plans more closely, you will be reminded of the three types of days you'll find during this part of your plan:

1. **"B" cycle day is your baseline day.** These are the days you are meeting the body's perceived needs expressed as PER (perceived efficiency rate), which you learned about previously. That line of PER gives your body what it needs when it needs it, so the body doesn't have to go into survival mode.

2. **"C" cycle day is carb-down day.** These are days when you reduce calories and carbohydrates and the days you are actually using up excess stored fat.

3. **"D" cycle day is carb-up day.** People smile when they see this day. This is when you increase carb intake at the end of your

day, to maximize your metabolism and replace higher amounts of the hormones that help you burn fat.

FAT-LOSS FACT

The more often the body learns to "go find fat," the easier and easier it gets to crack the code.

Rules for the Macro-Patterning Cycle

Keep in mind the following guidelines for the Macro-Patterning Cycle:

• Keep track of what you're taking in every day. Use the log sheets found in Chapter 11 or order the ForeverFit log book from our website to keep track, because that way, you can see what you're eating and doing.

• Eat every three to four hours up until two hours before bed.

• You must have a minimum of four meals each day; five small meals are preferred.

• Limit portion size to the size of your fist. When you're eating out, ask for a to-go container at the beginning of the meal, and portion-control your food.

• Drink your minimum water amount per day. For women, that's 70 to 80 ounces; for men, it's 100 to 128 ounces per day.

• Eat foods on the meal plans for the Macro-Patterning Cycle or from the substitution food lists found on the following pages.

- Continue to eat your broccoli daily. But you don't have to eat broccoli on carb-up days.

- Don't eat any protein bars or fake no-carb or low-carb prepackaged foods.

- Alcohol is best resumed on carb-up days and only after the third week on the program.

- Don't force meals or eat too much at each meal. A good rule of thumb is that if you get to the next meal without feeling hungry, the previous meal was too much. If you are starving before it's time to eat again, then the previous meal was not enough.

- Plan for Food Passes. For special birthdays, holidays, or other special events when you need to have a carb-up or cheat meal, make sure that you arrange your days to have a carb-down day the day before. If you wind up indulging yourself, schedule a carb-down day for the day after as well.

- Begin to exercise. You need to make exercise a habit after you've been through the Carb-Deplete Cycle and have more routine—and energy—in your life. Remember, to accelerate fat loss, you must create an energy deficit, which can be accomplished in one of two ways: by reducing calories or by exercising. Most likely, the meal plans you're following are already reducing the calories you used to eat, so the only way left to you now to create an energy deficit is to exercise.

Code Cracker

Limit your portion size to the size of your fist. (When eating out, ask for a to-go container at the beginning of the meal, and portion-control your food.)

Weekly Meal Plans for the Macro-Patterning Cycle

During week 2, you will begin to bring most of the foods that you consume regularly back into your daily meals. You will see less rigidity in the meal plans—and more substitutions. For best results, it is recommended that you continue to abstain from alcohol on carb-up days this week.

Week 2 Meal Plan

Planners B, C, D	Mon Day 8	Tues Day 9	Wed Day 10	Thurs Day 11	Fri Day 12	Sat Day 13	Sun Day 14
Cycle Day	C	C	B	B	C	D	B
Starch Amount	1 time before 3:00 P.M.	1 time before 3:00 P.M.	2 times before 3:00 P.M.	2 times before 3:00 P.M.	1 time before 3:00 P.M.	Last 2 meals	2 times before 3:00 P.M.

During week 3, you will have two carb-up days, on Wednesday and Saturday. After this week is the best time to add in sweets and alcohol on carb-up days.

Week 3 Meal Plan

Planners B, C, D	Mon Day 15	Tues Day 16	Wed Day 17	Thurs Day 18	Fri Day 19	Sat Day 20	Sun Day 21
Cycle Day	B	C	D	B	C	D	B
Starch Amount	2 times before 3:00 P.M.	1 time before 3:00 P.M.	Last 2 meals	2 times before 3:00 P.M.	1 time before 3:00 P.M.	Last 2 meals	2 times before 3:00 P.M.

Now that you're at week 4, you've made it through 21 days! Your body will now begin the change that will put you on the path to good health for life. The fourth week is the last week in your Macro-Patterning Cycle. In this week you will begin to introduce back to your meal plans some goodies and alcohol.

Week 4 Meal Plan

Planners B, C, D	Mon Day 22	Tues Day 23	Wed Day 24	Thurs Day 25	Fri Day 26	Sat Day 27	Sun Day 28
Cycle Day	B	C	D	B	C	D	B
Starch Amount	2 times before 3:00 P.M.	1 time before 3:00 P.M.	Last 2 meals	2 times before 3:00 P.M.	1 time before 3:00 P.M.	Last 2 meals	2 times before 3:00 P.M.

Substitution Food Lists for the Macro-Patterning Cycle, Accelerated Fat-Loss Cycle, and Maintenance Cycle

The following food substitution lists can be used for the Macro-Patterning Cycle, Accelerated Fat-Loss Cycle, and Maintenance Cycle.

Type P = Protein Requirements and Substitutions
- Consume protein at each meal, at least four times per day. Five meals are ideal.
- Consume the amount of protein listed on the meal planner. An estimate is OK, but weighing your food after it is cooked is best. Remember, protein amounts are based on cooked weight. When you order out, the menu lists the weight precooked. Meat cooks down by an ounce or two.

  - Chicken breast
  - Cottage cheese
  - Egg whites or egg substitute
  - Fresh fish: salmon, trout, etc.
  - Lean beef
  - Protein shake
  - Tuna
  - Turkey breast
- Cottage cheese may be consumed only once per day.
- If you are consuming a protein shake, use a shake with 1 gram sugar or less and carbs under 6 grams. Adjust the serving for not more than 25 grams (approximately 3 to 4 ounces) of protein for women and 40 grams (approximately 5 to 8 ounces) for men.
- When eating egg whites, you may have 1 whole egg with your whites, if desired.

Type S = Starchy Carbohydrate Requirements and Substitutions

- Consume *only* the following starchy carbs and in the specified amounts.
  - Black or red beans; lentils (½ cup cooked)
  - Oatmeal (½ cup dry measure)
  - Cream of Rice or Wheat (1 serving per package label)
  - Ezekiel bread—flourless bread or millet bread (2 slices)
  - Grits (1 serving per package label)
  - Potato, any kind (½ medium, 1 small, or 6–8 ounces)
  - Rice (½ cup cooked)
- On carb-down days, consume one starch with a protein before 3:00 P.M.
- On baseline days, consume two starches with a protein before 3:00 P.M.

Type V = Vegetable Requirements and Substitutions

- You may consume the following listed foods in unlimited quantities with proteins or a meal. Don't snack between meals on veggies.
  - Asparagus
  - Broccoli
  - Cabbage
  - Celery
  - Lettuce
  - Mushrooms
  - Radicchio
  - Radishes
  - Spinach
- You may consume any other veggies not listed in minimum (1 cup) quantities.
- Do not eat carrots, corn, peas, or beets except on carb-up days.

Type O = Fat Requirements and Substitutions

- Consume *one* serving of the following "A" fats one to two times daily.
  - Canola oil
  - Essential fatty acid supplement
  - Flaxseed oil
  - Olive oil
- Minimize "B" (bad) fats to under 20 grams per day. These are saturated or nonbeneficial fats.
  - Butter
  - Cheese
  - Fatty red meat
  - Mayonnaise
  - Salad dressing
- Limit the amount of fat you eat at meals containing starchy carbs.

Type A = Fruit Requirements and Substitutions

- You may have one serving of any of the following fresh fruits when indicated on your meal planner.
  - Apple (1 medium)
  - Banana (1 medium)
  - Berries, any kind (1 cup)
  - Cantaloupe (½)
  - Grapefruit (½)
  - Grapes (1 cup)
  - Orange (1 medium)
  - Peach (1 medium)
  - Tangerine (1 medium)

Type SA = Sweets and Alcohol Requirements and Substitutions

- The following list provides examples of the types of foods you can have for type SA. For sweets and alcohol marked by an asterisk (*), it is best to wait to consume these foods until after the third week, as indicated on your meal planner. All of the other starches listed may be consumed on any carb-up day when indicated on your meal planner.
  - Alcohol*
  - Bagel
  - Beets
  - Bread
  - Cake*
  - Carrots
  - Chips and snacks
  - Corn
  - Crackers
  - French fries
  - Ice cream*
  - Pasta
  - Pizza
  - Sugary pastries*

- For best fat-loss results, limit alcohol consumption to one of the carb-up days per week.
- It's recommended that persons with diabetes not consume alcohol at any time.

Type FF = Free-Food Requirements and Substitutions

- Consume free food as a complement to a meal, not as a meal. (However, you can have flavored gelatin or a Fudgesicle as an evening snack on baseline days where indicated on your meal planner.) If hunger is an issue, then choose a protein instead.
  - Artificial sweetener
  - Sugar-free coffee
  - Crystal Light drink mix
  - Diet soda
  - Fudgesicle (1)
  - Hot sauce
  - Lemon
  - Lime
  - Mustard
  - Nonstick cooking spray
  - Powdered spices
  - Reddi-wip spray cream (1 serving)
  - Soy sauce
  - Sugar-free gelatin (1 serving)
  - Sugar-free tea
  - Vinegar
  - Worcestershire sauce

Sample Daily Meal Plans for the Macro-Patterning Cycle

Macro-Patterning Cycle Meal Plan B: Sample Baseline Day

MEAL	TYPE	WOMEN	MEN
1	P/S	**Wendy's Crepe** (See page 116.)	**Wendy's Crepe** (See page 116.)
2	P	½ cup cottage cheese	30–40 g protein shake (requirements on food substitution list)
3	P/S/V	**Wendy's Turkey Burgers on Un-Buns** (See page 135.)	**Wendy's Turkey Burgers on Un-Buns** (See page 135.)
4	P/O	Chocolate raspberry shake: 20–25 g chocolate protein powder added to 10–12 oz. premade Crystal Light raspberry drink.	Chocolate raspberry shake: 20–25 g chocolate protein powder added to 10–12 oz. premade Crystal Light raspberry drink.p
104	P/V/O	4–6 oz. seared chicken with Cajun spices 1 cup green beans with garlic Salad with tomato, cucumber, and 1 tbsp. extra-virgin olive oil and vinegar or low-calorie, low-sugar dressing	6–8 oz. seared chicken with Cajun spices 1 cup green beans with garlic Salad with tomato, cucumber, and 1 tbsp. extra-virgin olive oil and vinegar or low-calorie, low-sugar dressing
6	FF	1 serving sugar-free gelatin with 1 tbsp. Reddi-wip spray cream (not Cool Whip)	1 serving sugar-free gelatin with 1 tbsp. Reddi-wip spray cream (not Cool Whip)

Type Key

P = Protein S = Starch V = Vegetable O = Fat FF = Free Food

Notes

1. This sample food plan shows five meals and a sixth free-food meal. If you consume only four meals, you may skip meal 2 or 4, for a total of four meals that day.

2. Make sure to consume one starch in two different meals before 3:00 P.M.

3. If you would like to substitute a different food at any particular meal, you must follow the type listed next to that meal and substitute the same type of food from your substitution list.

Your Notes

_____

_____

_____

_____

_____

_____

_____

Macro-Patterning Cycle Meal Plan C:
Sample Carb-Down Day (Starch at Breakfast)

MEAL	TYPE	WOMEN	MEN
1	P/S	**Power Oats** (See page 117.)	**Power Oats** (See page 117.)
2	P	½ cup cottage cheese (2 percent fat)	1 cup cottage cheese (2 percent fat)
3	P/V/O	Tomato stuffed with 3–4 oz. tuna, dill, and diced celery Salad with cucumber and 1 tbsp. extra-virgin olive oil and vinegar	Tomato stuffed with 6–8 oz. tuna, dill, and diced celery Salad with cucumber and 1 tbsp. extra-virgin olive oil and vinegar
4	P/O	Crispy lettuce wrap: 2–3 oz. turkey breast and cheese rolled with fresh romaine leaves	Chocolate shake: 30–40 g chocolate protein powder blended with 10–12 oz. water and ice for desired thickness
5	P/V/O	4 oz. filet mignon 1 cup broccoli Salad with tomato, cucumber, and 1 tbsp. extra-virgin olive oil and vinegar or low-calorie, low-sugar dressing	6–8 oz. filet mignon 1 cup broccoli Salad with tomato, cucumber, and 1 tbsp. extra-virgin olive oil and vinegar or low-calorie, low-sugar dressing
6	P	**Orange Dream Protein Shake** (See page 89.)	**Orange Dream Protein Shake** (See page 89.)

Type Key
P = Protein S = Starch V = Vegetable O = Fat

Notes

1. This sample food plan shows six meals. If you consume only four meals, you may skip meal 2 or 4 and meal 6, for a total of four meals that day.

2. If you consume only five meals, you may skip meal 2 or 4 or 6, for a total of five meals.

3. If you would like to substitute a different food at any particular meal, you must follow the type listed next to that meal and substitute the same type of food from your substitution list.

4. Make sure to eat one starch in one meal before 3:00 P.M.

Your Notes

_____

_____

_____

_____

_____

_____

_____

Macro-Patterning Cycle Meal Plan C:
Sample Carb-Down Day (Starch at Lunch)

MEAL	TYPE	WOMEN	MEN
1	P/O	**Mushroom and Spinach Omelet** (See page 88.)	**Mushroom and Spinach Omelet** (See page 88.)
2	P	½ cup cottage cheese	Vanilla shake: 30–40 g vanilla protein powder blended with 10–12 oz. water and ice for desired thickness
3	P/S/V	3–4 oz. grilled chicken with lemon and Italian herb seasoning 1 cup broccoli ½ cup cooked rice	6–8 oz. grilled chicken with lemon and Italian herb seasoning 1 cup broccoli ¾ cup cooked rice
4	P	Crispy lettuce wrap: 3–4 oz. turkey breast and 1–2 slices cheese rolled in large Bibb lettuce leaf with mustard or light mayonnaise	Crispy lettuce wrap: 6 oz. turkey breast and 2 slices cheese rolled in large Bibb lettuce leaf with mustard or light mayonnaise
5	P/V/O	4–6 oz. broiled salmon or halibut 1 cup steamed asparagus Salad with tomato, cucumber, and 1 tbsp. extra-virgin olive oil and vinegar or low-calorie, low-sugar dressing	8 oz. broiled salmon or halibut 1 cup steamed asparagus Salad with tomato, cucumber, and 1 tbsp. extra-virgin olive oil and vinegar or low-calorie, low-sugar dressing
6	P	Chocolate shake: 20–25 g chocolate protein powder blended with 6–8 oz. water and ice for desired thickness	Chocolate shake: 30–40 g chocolate protein powder blended with 10–12 oz. water and ice for desired thickness

Type Key
P = Protein S = Starch V = Vegetable O = Fat

Notes

1. This sample food plan shows six meals. If you consume only four meals, you may skip meal 2 or 4 and meal 6, for a total of four meals that day.

2. If you consume only five meals, you may skip meal 2 or 4 or 6, for a total of five meals.

3. If you would like to substitute a different food at any particular meal, you must follow the type listed next to that meal and substitute the same type of food from your substitution list.

4. Make sure to eat one starch in one meal before 3:00 P.M.

Your Notes

_____

_____

_____

_____

_____

_____

_____

_____

Macro-Patterning Cycle Meal Plan D: Sample Carb-Up Day (Nondiabetic)

MEAL	TYPE	WOMEN	MEN
1	P/S	Eggs on a bagel: 1 whole egg plus 2–3 egg whites, scrambled and served on ½ bagel	Eggs on a bagel: 1 whole egg plus 4–5 egg whites, scrambled and served on 1 bagel
2	P/A	½ cup cottage cheese with any fruit	Vanilla shake: 30–40 g vanilla protein powder blended with 10–12 oz. water and ice for desired thickness
3	P/V/O	Chicken Caesar salad: 3–4 oz. chicken on large lettuce and cucumber salad with 1 tbsp. extra-virgin olive oil and vinegar (croutons OK)	Chicken Caesar salad: 6–8 oz. chicken on large lettuce and cucumber salad with 1 tbsp. extra-virgin olive oil and vinegar (croutons OK)
4	SA or A	6-in. roast beef and Swiss sub sandwich on wheat bread 1 small bag chips	6-in. roast beef and Swiss sub sandwich on wheat bread 1 small bag chips
5	SA	1–2 slices pepperoni pizza— meat OK, but no extra cheese (*Don't stuff!*)	2–3 slices pepperoni pizza— meat OK, but no extra cheese (*Don't stuff!*)

Type Key

P = Protein S = Starch V = Vegetable O = Fat A = Fruit SA = Sweets and Alcohol

Notes

1. The preceding food plan is a carb-up meal for a person without diabetes. If, after trying this plan, you feel lethargic or sickly, you may be carb-sensitive, and the following diabetic carb-up plan may work better for you.

2. This sample food plan shows five meals. If you consume only four meals, you may skip meal 2.

3. If you aren't exercising, have only one carb-up meal as the last meal of the day.

4. Sweets, starches, and alcohol are allowable after day 7. However, for the best results, do not eat these foods until after day 21.

5. Don't overeat at your carb-up meal. Eat until you are satisfied, not stuffed.

6. If you would like to substitute a different food at any particular meal, you must follow the type listed next to that meal and substitute the same type of food from your substitution list.

Your Notes

_____

_____

_____

_____

_____

_____

_____

Macro-Patterning Cycle Meal Plan D:
Sample Carb-Up Day (Diabetic)

MEAL	TYPE	WOMEN	MEN
1	P/S	Eggs on a bagel: 1 whole egg plus 2–3 egg whites, scrambled and served on ½ bagel	Eggs on a bagel: 1 whole egg and 4–5 egg whites, scrambled and served on 1 bagel
2	P/O	½ cup cottage cheese	Vanilla shake: 30–40 g vanilla protein powder blended with 10–12 oz. water and ice for desired thickness
3	P/SA	6-in. smoked turkey and Muenster sandwich on wheat bread 1 small bag chips	6-in. smoked turkey and Muenster sandwich on wheat bread 1 small bag chips
4	P/SA	Crispy lettuce wrap: 2–3 oz. turkey breast and cheese rolled with fresh romaine lettuce leaf Fresh strawberries or cantaloupe	Vanilla shake with berries or banana: 30–40 g vanilla protein powder blended with 10–12 oz. water and ice for desired thickness
5	SA	Herbed chicken penne pasta (any combination of pasta, sauce, and herbs) 1 crusty roll (Don't stuff!)	Herbed chicken penne pasta (any combination of pasta, sauce, and herbs) 1 crusty roll (Don't stuff!)

Type Key

P = Protein   S = Starch   O = Fat   A = Fruit   SA = Sweets and Alcohol

Notes

1. The preceding food plan is a carb-up day for a person with diabetes. The idea is to have small amounts of carbs through your day with protein. Individuals who do not have diabetes but are sensitive to carbs also may prefer using this plan.

2. This plan shows five meals. If you consume only four meals, you may skip meal 2.

3. Sweets and alcohol are allowable after day 7. However, for the best results, do not include them until after day 21. People with diabetes should avoid these types of foods for better long-term balance of blood sugar.

4. Don't overeat at meals. Eat until satisfied, not stuffed.

5. If you would like to substitute a different food at any particular meal, you must follow the type listed next to that meal and substitute the same type of food from your substitution list.

Your Notes

_____

_____

_____

_____

_____

_____

_____

_____

Wendy's Top-Five Macro-Patterning Shopping List Items

Many of us take shopping for granted, believing the mega-food companies' claims that "low fat," "reduced fat," "no fat," "reduced calorie," "calorie free," and "healthy choice" really mean what they say. Once you learn to crack the fat-loss code, however, you never quite look at the grocery store the same way again.

I always feel like I'm under attack in the market, like I have to dodge the advertising and product placement of all these so-called "healthy choices" just to get to the real food. So I thought it would be helpful to share my own top-five list of carb-deplete foods that I buy in addition to what's on my carb-deplete list. The best part is, now that we can add other foods back in, I have a few favorites:

1. **Quaker quick oats:** If you look in my pantry, you will always see a canister of quick oats. This is a fantastic moder-ate-glycemic carbohydrate and also quick to prepare and very transportable. I tell my clients not to mess with the finely milled instant packets, because you miss out on the great fiber benefits oatmeal has to offer. Instead, make your own "instant." Buy the large canister, measure half a cup, and put it in a baggy or plastic container with a lid. Stir in a few packets of sugar substi-tute and some cinnamon powder (not cinnamon sugar). When you're ready to make breakfast, all you need is some water and a microwave oven. Here is a great meal tip: After preparing your oatmeal, add 1 scoop of vanilla protein powder, and stir it in. Now you have a protein and starch (P/S) meal combined. When mixing it together, just add a little more water so as not to have your oatmeal too stiff.

2. **Ezekiel bread:** Made by Food for Life, this is flourless, organic bread that you will find in the freezer section of your local grocery store. If you're having trouble tracking it down, check their website, foodforlife.com, for a store that carries it

near you. My favorite variety is sesame, but they have a seven-grain and even a low-sodium bread. All are yummy, and some stores even carry their tortilla wraps and pita pockets, too. This bread is allowed on carb-down and baseline days, which makes it convenient for making a sandwich or enjoying toast with your eggs.

3. **Sweet potato:** This is my favorite kind of potato, and it's absolutely packed with a lot of fantastic nutrients. Each week I bake several potatoes in the oven all at once, but they can easily be microwaved quickly, too, and they keep well for several days in the refrigerator.

4. **Rice:** Great news, rice lovers: on the Nutrition Boot Camp plan, any type of rice is allowed on any day, so it doesn't matter whether you have brown or white rice. I especially like sushi, so most of the time I eat my rice in a sushi roll, and I typically ask for it to be made with half the rice. I have also put leftover cold rice in my salad for a starch when I didn't have a way to heat a meal.

5. **Sugar-free Jell-O:** If you still need a little sweet dessert taste, this dessert is allowed on baseline days, but not on carb-down days. It is even OK to add some Reddi-wip whip cream on top (not Cool Whip), but be cautious; spray whipped cream still has calories.

Wendy's "Mmm Good" Favorite Recipes for the Macro-Patterning Cycle

Here are some more of my favorite, "Mmm Good" recipes. Enjoy!

Wendy's Crepes

Use planners B, C, D

> 1 whole egg plus 3 egg whites
>
> ¼ to ½ cup oatmeal
>
> 2 packets sugar substitute
>
> 1 heaping scoop protein powder
>
> 2 tablespoons water

Place egg and egg whites, oatmeal, sugar substitute, and protein powder in a bowl; combine and add water as needed to make a smooth batter. Add to skillet like pancakes (or just make one big pancake), and cover the skillet with a lid. Let it set up, and then flip. Turn off heat, and put the lid back on until finished cooking. I add cinnamon on top, or you can (sparingly) use sugar-free syrup or low-sugar jam.

1 serving

Nutritional Value
Protein: 20 grams
Fat: 1 gram
Carbs: 15–25 grams

Power Oats

Use planners B, C, D

> 1 serving quick or old-fashioned oats
>
> 1–1½ scoops vanilla protein powder
>
> 2 packets sugar substitute
>
> Cinnamon and/or low-sugar jam

Prepare oats according to directions, usng a little extra added water. When oats are cooked, stir in protein powder, sugar substitute, and low-sugar jam or lots of cinnamon.

1 serving

Nutritional Value
Protein: 20–35 grams
Fat: 1 gram
Carbs: 25 grams

Broccoli and Rice Salad

Use planners B and D

½ cup cooked rice

½ cup cooked broccoli

5 crushed almonds or walnuts

Dressing

1 tablespoon extra-virgin olive oil

1 tablespoon balsamic vinegar

1 teaspoon Worcestershire sauce

½ package sugar substitute

In a large bowl, combine all dressing ingredients. Mix in rice, broccoli, and almonds, combining well until all ingredients are coated well with dressing.

Note: Add red pepper flakes if you like it a little hot. You can add orange segments—only on carb-up days—or turkey bacon, using the minimum amount.

1 serving

Nutritional Value
Protein: 1 gram
Fats: 4 grams
Carbs: 30 grams

Sesame Broccoli

Use planners B, C, D

> 1 tablespoon sesame seeds
>
> 1 tablespoon lemon juice
>
> 1 tablespoon soy sauce
>
> ½ teaspoon salt
>
> 1 10-ounce package frozen or 1 pound fresh
>   broccoli, cooked and drained

Preheat oven to 350°F. Spread sesame seeds on cookie sheet, and heat in oven for 5–10 minutes or until brown. Combine lemon juice, soy sauce, salt, and sesame seeds in a small pan. Heat to boiling. Pour over broccoli, coating all spears.

4 servings

Nutritional Value
Protein: 3 grams
Fat: 1 gram
Carbs: 4 grams

Citrus Grilled Chicken

Use planners B, C, D

> 6 medium boneless, skinless chicken breast halves
>
> ¼ cup balsamic vinegar
>
> ¾ teaspoon garlic powder
>
> ¼ teaspoon pepper
>
> 3 tablespoons lime juice
>
> 3 tablespoons lemon juice
>
> 3 tablespoons Dijon mustard

Place chicken in shallow dish. Combine remaining ingredients; pour over chicken. Cover and refrigerate 4 hours or overnight. Drain marinade. Grill chicken over high heat or on hot coals, turning once for about 4 to 5 minutes on each side.

6 servings

Nutritional Value
Protein: 27 grams
Fat: 3 grams
Carbs: 7 grams

Sesame Chicken with Wasabi Marinade

Use planners B and D

> 6 medium boneless, skinless chicken breasts

Marinade

> ¼ cup sesame seeds, toasted
>
> 2 tablespoons extra-virgin olive oil
>
> 1 tablespoon Thai fish sauce
>
> 2 tablespoons rice wine vinegar
>
> 2 tablespoons or more toasted sesame oil
>
> 1 tablespoon brown sugar
>
> 2 tablespoons wasabi powder (available at Asian
>   markets)

Split chicken breasts through thickness. Pound chicken fillets evenly to about ¼ inch thick.

To make the marinade, toast the sesame seeds in a preheated heavy skillet on medium heat. Remove and grind slightly to release their flavor. In large bowl, combine olive oil, fish sauce, vinegar, and sesame oil. Add brown sugar and wasabi powder; mix well and then stir in sesame seeds.

Place the chicken in a sealable plastic bag, and add the marinade. Seal plastic bag, and turn several times for 30 minutes at room temperature. Preheat a skillet, and add some sesame oil. Lay the chicken in the skillet, and sauté without stirring for 2 minutes or until the edges begin to turn opaque. Flip chicken with tongs, and cook until just medium rare. Remove to a heated dish, and continue to cook additional chicken pieces until all are cooked. Slice chicken scaloppine style (2-inch-wide pieces cut at a 45-degree angle and against the grain). Spread on a serving platter; spoon marinade over the chicken, and keep warm until ready to serve.

6 servings

Nutritional Value
Protein: 27 grams
Fat: 6 grams
Carbs: 4 grams

"My Energy Level Has Tripled"
Lavonia Drawdy

I started Nutrition Boot Camp in September 2006. Since joining the program, I have lost ninety-five pounds! The diet has changed my life and gave me a lifestyle that I could enjoy. I often enjoyed southern cooking and all the fried foods that go along with it, but now that I understand more about my body, I have been able to limit those fried foods and actually enjoy a more healthy way of eating.

I was able to follow this program through the holidays. Even when I traveled, I was still able to maintain my weight during that time, or even lose a few pounds. I lived a sedentary lifestyle because my body always hurt and ached; now I can say I keep up with my family and friends on any outing. My energy level has tripled. I can walk for great

lengths without pain. I would never have imagined doing any weight training, but I enjoy it. I truly feel stronger and younger.

I can't thank Wendy and ForeverFit enough for changing my life. Wendy has been wonderful; she literally saved my life. She believes in you, and her program is well-guided and instructional. When you can learn how your body works, it makes a difference in the way you feed it. My blood work is normal, and I have been able to reduce my blood pressure medications after years of struggling.

7

Cycle 3

Accelerated Fat Loss Cycle, Weeks 5–6

The adaptive response is your body's means to survive. You need to accelerate the fat-loss cycle to break this pattern. The reason this is an eight-week process and not, say, a two-week process is that the body is continually learning to adapt. Even though this may be the first time you've ever macro-patterned, the body is very good at adapting.

As we manipulate energy stores with baseline, carb-up, or carb-down days, the body is sneakily trying to find a way not to go grab fat. The body is far from lazy. As a matter of fact, it is a workhorse—constantly working to store more and more to ensure its survival. It gets in its pattern and becomes so good at streamlining the fat-storing process that it is like the best employee coming up with continual systems to make your job much easier.

We all want security and comfort; the body is no different. The body loves and wants to feel secure the way we do. We like what feels comfortable: our surroundings, our family, even our favorite blanket. Well, the body likes to be comfortable, too. But as we all know, the comfort zone isn't always the *Crack the Fat-Loss Code* zone. To keep the body on its toes, we have to shock it from time to time and manipulate it even further. That's what weeks 5 and 6 are all about.

Weeks 5 and 6 are very tricky for the body because, typically, this is where most diets fail. We can do most things for a month, even starve ourselves. Eat less, work out more, drink less, drink more, cut carbs, add protein. We can do it—until we can't do it anymore. But by week 5 of any fat-loss program, the body has learned our tricks; it has identified our patterns. It wants to adapt, and it does so by reserving and conserving energy, draining our energy levels, lowering our resistance to disease, and storing fat.

To keep the body from falling back into old patterns and adapting, and to avoid hitting the diet plateau, we change the cycle, using the same three days as before—baseline, carb-up, and carb-down days—only we're going to shift things around a little. Remember that the only way to alter the body's point of adaptation is through force of will. We have to change it; it won't change on its own. To effect that change, we're going to start having two carb-down days in a row. This will be reflected in your meal plan. It's a way to follow up and ensure that your body is forced to go find fat as an energy source.

> ### 🔒 Code Cracker
> To keep the body from adapting and avoid hitting the diet plateau, we change the cycle, using the same three days as before.

Consider this a "mini carb deplete" to shock the body out of its point of adaptation, which tends to get "stuck" if we're not careful. We're just changing the cycle up a bit to keep the body on its toes.

In the plan that you followed during weeks 3 and 4, Tuesdays and Fridays were carb-down days, so you're already in the habit of scheduling these days each week. These days are already in place. To accelerate fat loss, you will double up. In essence, you do two in a row, so you're sucking some—but not all—of those glycogen stores down a little. Force your body to look for fat stores for energy. So pick either Monday or Thursday to carb down, too.

At this point, you should be feeling good and motivated, so this should be a good time for you to double up. You should be exercising now, losing weight, fitting in your clothes better. Keep track! Write down your progress, and post it on the fridge. I asked for eight weeks, and you're almost there—five, then six weeks down and counting. It feels great when you have the control and confidence of getting your life back.

Code Cracker

Consider this cycle a "mini carb deplete" to shock the body out of its point of adaptation, which tends to get "stuck" if you're not careful.

Rules for the Accelerated Fat-Loss Cycle

Now that the changes are beginning to show, let's pick up the pace a little. This two-week cycle is a little more challenging than the previous three-week cycle, but it's not as stringent as the Carb-Deplete Cycle was. Because of your body's adaptive response, no one cycle should ever last more than three weeks without changes. The changes we are going to make will accelerate your fat loss. You should use the Accelerated Fat-Loss Cycle for only a maximum of two weeks. Along the way, remember to continue exercising, be positive, and enjoy the process.

By this point, you should understand each day pretty well, and you may already have a plan for the foods you like on certain days. Your family and friends now also join in with knowing your days. Congratulations! You have already begun to make the lifestyle change that will keep you fit and healthy to live your life the way you choose. After you are finished with this cycle, I will discuss how you proceed from here. Remember to say thanks to all the people who are beginning to compliment you on your weight loss and healthy glow.

You'll notice now that the rules lists are getting shorter; that's because you should know them by now. Still, it's always good to go "back to school," kind of like your body's doing right now. So here are some reminders to keep you on track:

- Write down everything that goes in your mouth, so you know what you are consuming.
- Eat every three to four hours up until two hours before bed.
- You must have a minimum of four meals each day; five small meals are preferred.
- Limit your portion size to the size of your fist.
- Follow your type key for each day, and substitute if desired from the macro-patterning substitution list in Chapter 6.
- Drink your minimum water amount per day.
- Eat foods on the meal planner for the Accelerated Fat-Loss Cycle or from the substitution food lists.
- Continue to eat as much broccoli as you can for all the great nutritional value it delivers.
- Consume alcohol in moderation on carb-up days.
- Don't force meals or eat too much at each meal.

Code Cracker

Congratulations! You have already begun to make the lifestyle change that will keep you fit and healthy to live your life the way you choose.

"I Got in Shape for the Biggest Battle of My Life"
Denise Charlesworth

At the age of twenty-nine, I was at least fifteen to twenty pounds overweight. Because of my genetics, I felt that this was going to be the weight I would continue to carry. However, unbeknownst to me, through a blood test during a routine physical exam, I found out I had hypothyroidism. Well, once I started on medication for hypothyroidism and without even trying, I dropped ten pounds. Wow, this was great! Not only did I love the fact that my clothes were sagging on me, I felt better physically and emotionally. Of course, I wanted to lose even more weight.

Before long, I took an interest in exercising every day at home, using Jane Fonda and other exercise videos. Eventually, I found myself joining a gym and becoming addicted to weight training and cardio. Because I wanted to become leaner and drop more body fat, I signed up with a personal trainer. After giving a couple of trainers a whirl, I felt that I was really getting nowhere. While I was getting more tone, I was not losing any more fat.

Then I noticed someone in my gym who was extremely lean and had great-looking biceps and shoulders. I definitely was envious. Why can't I look like that? I struck up a conversation to find out what her secret was, and Wendy Chant's name came up. So, what do I have to lose? More fat, I hope!

(continued)

I called Wendy and set up an appointment with her. As I sat and listened to her, I was so impressed with not only her knowledge of the body and how it reacts once food is consumed, but her total enthusiasm in teaching the whole concept. I was hooked!

Wendy weighed me in at 118 pounds; my body fat was 16 percent. For the next six months, she monitored my meals, and I weight-trained with her once a week. I also did some form of cardio six to seven days a week and weight-trained another two to three days on my own.

Before long, I noticed that my arms were looking lean and sleek. My biggest problem area, saddlebags on my hips, was just about gone. My legs never looked that thin, even when I was a teen. Wendy had me, at the age of forty-four, in the best shape of my life! My weight dropped to 111 pounds, and body fat dropped to 10 percent. I was lean, tight, and mean and wanted to train for a show.

Then life changed just that fast. One and a half months after my annual mammogram (which was normal), I felt two lumps in my right breast. Although they were tender (and early-stage cancer supposedly does not hurt), I called my gynecologist. He immediately had me schedule an ultrasound. After that, everything happened really fast. Suspicious mass led to a biopsy. Results came back positive. I opted for just a lumpectomy. Unfortunately, the pathology reports indicated ten positive lymph nodes out of twenty-two and lots of little tumors starting under the current tumors.

On Valentine's Day 2002, four days after my forty-fifth birthday, I was back in the hospital to have a bilateral mastectomy and reconstruction performed. What lay ahead of me were eight rounds of chemo and thirty-three rounds of radiation, plus weekly visits to various doctors.

Through it all, God gave me a huge amount of strength that I never knew I had. With everything I had to endure, I still kept up with my workouts all through chemo. I continued to go to the gym, even when all my hair fell out. I either donned a scarf or kept my wig on! Although my workouts were not as strenuous as when I was training with Wendy, I would still pretend that she was in the back of the gym watching me, so I wouldn't slack! Her encouragement also kept me going.

Bottom line, because I was in good shape and continued with my workouts, a clean food plan, and supplementation as I had been taught, I was able to get through chemo better than most. I did have the few days of nausea and fatigue, but I didn't have so much of the side effects that most cancer patients experience. My body was able to recover and repair relatively quickly. To date, I have been cancer free for five and a half years. Considering my type of cancer, my doctors are thrilled. Thank you, Wendy, for all you taught me!

Weekly Meal Plans for the Accelerated Fat-Loss Cycle

To substitute foods during the Accelerated Fat-Loss Cycle, use the substitution lists provided in Chapter 6.

Week 5 Meal Planner

Planners B, C, D	Mon Day 29	Tues Day 30	Wed Day 31	Thurs Day 32	Fri Day 33	Sat Day 34	Sun Day 35
Cycle Day	C	C	D	B	C	D	B
Starch Amount	1 time before 3:00 P.M.	1 time before 3:00 P.M.	Last 2 meals	2 times before 3:00 P.M.	1 time before 3:00 P.M.	Last 2 meals	2 times before 3:00 P.M.

Week 6 Meal Planner

Planners B, C, D	Mon Day 36	Tues Day 37	Wed Day 38	Thurs Day 39	Fri Day 40	Sat Day 41	Sun Day 42
Cycle Day	C	C	D	B	C	D	B
Starch Amount	1 time before 3:00 P.M.	1 time before 3:00 P.M.	Last 2 meals	2 times before 3:00 P.M.	1 time before 3:00 P.M.	Last 2 meals	2 times before 3:00 P.M.

Wendy's "Mmm Good" Favorite Recipes for the Accelerated Fat-Loss Cycle

Since there is one extra carb-down day in your week now, here is my favorite chicken recipe that you can choose to make and enjoy on those days. For more "Mmm Good" choices, refer to Chapter 12.

Wendy's Bull's-Eye Breakfast

Use planners B, C, D

1 slice Ezekiel bread

1 whole egg plus 4 egg whites

Pepper

Lightly toast bread. Cut out a small round hole in the center of the bread, and place the remaining slice in a hot, greased skillet. (Save bread cutout scraps for another use.) Crack the whole egg into the hole, and pour additional egg whites over the top. Flip carefully to keep the yolk intact; cook until done. Grind pepper to taste. Just like Mom used to make!

1 serving

Nutritional Value
Protein: 19 grams
Fat: 3 grams
Carbs: 12 grams

Rachel's Balsamic Grilled Chicken

Use planners B, C, D

> Newman's Own Balsamic Vinaigrette salad dressing,
> enough to cover chicken in bowl
>
> 2 packets sugar substitute
>
> 4 medium boneless, skinless chicken breast halves
>
> 1 teaspoon dried rosemary

Pour salad dressing into a shallow dish, and stir in sugar substitute. Place chicken in dish, making sure it is almost completely covered. Sprinkle with rosemary. Cover and refrigerate at least 1 hour; about 4 hours is best. Remove chicken from marinade, and grill over high heat or hot coals, turning once, for about 4 to 5 minutes on each side.

4 servings

Nutritional Value
Protein: 27 grams
Fat: 1 gram
Carbs: 1 gram

Wendy's Turkey Burgers on Un-Buns

Use planners B, C, D

> 4 large portobello mushroom caps
>
> 1 tablespoon extra-virgin olive oil
>
> 1 1-pound package ground turkey breast (I use
> hormone- and antibiotic-free)
>
> Italian herb seasoning, optional
>
> Baby spinach leaves
>
> 1 tomato, diced

Preheat oven to 400°F, and prepare grill. Arrange mushrooms in a baking dish, and brush with olive oil. Bake 12 minutes. Season ground turkey with Italian herbs, if desired, and shape into four patties. Grill burgers, and place one on top of each mushroom cap. Place spinach and tomato on top.

4 servings

Nutritional Value
Protein: 27 grams
Fat: 1 gram
Carbs: 6 grams

8

Cycle 4

Maintenance Cycle, Weeks 7–8

Congratulations! You're at weeks 7 and 8. That means you've given me eight weeks of your life—and I've given you your life back. Let me rephrase that: you gave yourself your life back. This is a time for reflection and regrowth, a time for you to celebrate your accomplishments and set new goals for yourself.

Look how far you've come. Now decide where you'd like to go!

🔒 Code Cracker

Enjoy tasting your food again. Pay attention to what it feels like to have energy, vitality, and drive.

Look back over the plan, and revisit how you felt, coped with, and handled each week and cycle along the way. What were your stumbling points? High points? Low points? Remember that mistakes are only human; learning from mistakes is superhuman! Refamiliarize yourself with why each week and cycle worked and what it meant for your success.

These next two weeks are all about maintenance: maintaining your plan and getting even more familiar with the program. Discover new foods; create new recipes. Enjoy tasting your food again. Pay attention to what it feels like to have energy, vitality, and drive.

By now your body should be healing from years of abuse—abuse from too many calories, portions that were too big, and exercise sessions that weren't quite big enough. Use these two weeks to maintain your program and actually enjoy it!

The point of the Maintenance Cycle is to teach you, and your body, how to reintroduce more carbs into your lifestyle and readjust the pattern yet again. Remember that carb depletion is not an optimal way of life; it is a limited-use, temporary way to kick-start your body into resisting the adaptive response.

In fact, it is an unnatural state of being and unhealthy for more than seven days in a row and more than three times a year. So we can't naturally survive on such a strict, low-carb lifestyle. There is a specific time and place for it, and you've had that time and place. You can't stay there indefinitely, or it would do more harm than good.

The following three days will help guide you through this phase of the plan:

• **Maintenance baseline day:** You'll still have your baseline days; these will always be with you. But by now, you and the baseline days should be old friends. Get reacquainted! Remember, on maintenance baseline days, you can have fruit in the morning, but if you have diabetes, you should be cautious, because it may put your blood sugar off balance.

• **Cheat day:** During the designated cheat days, you can have foods not normally on the plan—any food you like. These include sugary carbs and alcohol. Just don't overeat.

- **High-carb day:** During high-carb days, you're having carbs through your day. Of course you're still learning and maintaining, so make sure to choose starches from the S category on your substitution list, not sugary carbs like doughnuts and cakes.

The biggest difference you'll notice in your meal plan is that during the Maintenance Cycle we're adding two new days, cheat day and high-carb day. But to accomplish that, you must have five baseline days in a row. Why? It's still a cycle, only now you're training the body to eat more carbs, not less.

You can put your cheat day and high-carb day in any order, before or after one another, as long as five maintenance baseline days are in a row. You need to keep the five baseline days in a row to maintain the cycle.

Although the Maintenance Cycle is a two-week increment in our eight-week pattern, you could follow it indefinitely. If you have already reached your fat-loss goals, you can stay on the Maintenance Cycle forever. If you haven't yet reached your fat-loss goals, the Maintenance Cycle is a great way to get grounded, reflect, look back on all your accomplishments, and even look ahead to what's next.

Give yourself and your body a break. Settle in and really get good at selecting the foods you like on your plan. By now, the newness should have worn off. Now is the time to truly stretch your wings and see how great life can be, now that you've cracked the fat-loss code and learned the secret to teaching your body, and not the other way around.

As you enjoy the natural benefits of eating smarter, everything should feel better. Your clothes might be too loose-fitting; get some new ones! Maybe you're confident enough in your exercise program to stop doing it by yourself and join a gym. Maybe you've gotten off a few of those prescription pills you thought you'd be on forever. Whatever goals you've reached so far, take this time to stop and celebrate.

Now it's time to look ahead and decide on your next goals. Have you reached your goals? Do you still have further to go? Decide and plan accordingly; don't proceed willy-nilly.

You've come too far to go back now.

Code Cracker

The point of the Maintenance Cycle is to teach you, and your body, how to reintroduce more carbs into your lifestyle and readjust the pattern yet again.

Rules for the Maintenance Cycle

You can't deplete, deny, or drain the body indefinitely. Even when you're doing smart things for your own body, it's still smart enough to find a way to reach that point of adaptation. The Maintenance Cycle is important to help reestablish a higher macronutrient profile for the body.

This cycle is specifically designed to help spark your metabolism, stop the adaptive response to a low-nutrient profile, and give you a planned break from dieting. Here are the specific rules—some new, some old—to help you get through the Maintenance Cycle:

- Use the Maintenance Cycle at the end of six or eight weeks.
- Make sure to have five maintenance baseline days in a row.
- Use the Maintenance Cycle for a minimum of two weeks or as long as you want to maintain your results.
- Write down everything that goes in your mouth, so you know what you are consuming. (But you don't need to log your cheat days.)

- Eat every three to four hours up until two hours before bed, except on cheat days, when no eating schedule is necessary.
- You must have a minimum of four meals each day, with five small meals preferred, except on cheat days.
- Limit your portion size to the size of your fist (except on cheat days).
- Follow your type key for each day, and substitute if desired from the list in Chapter 6.
- Drink your minimum amount of water every day.
- Consume alcohol in moderation on cheat days only.
- Don't overeat on cheat days.

Code Cracker

The Maintenance Cycle is important to help reestablish a higher macronutrient profile for the body.

Weekly Meal Plans for the Maintenance Cycle

Here you can find your current weekly meal plans for the Maintenance Cycle:

Meal Planner for Weeks 7 and 8

Planners B, CH, H	Mon	Tues	Wed	Thurs	Fri	Sat	Sun
Maintenance	B	B	B	B	B	CH	H

Sample Daily Meal Plans for the Maintenance Cycle

For food substitutions to use during the Maintenance Cycle, use the substitution lists in Chapter 6.

Maintenance Cycle Meal Plan B: Maintenance Baseline Day

MEAL	TYPE	WOMEN	MEN
1	P/S or A	Power oats: ½ cup oatmeal prepared with cinnamon and 2 packets sugar substitute; stir in 15–20 g protein powder (check label for protein amount)	Power oats: ¾ cup oatmeal prepared with cinnamon and 2 packets sugar substitute; stir in 20–30 g protein powder (check label for protein amount)
2	P or A	1 apple	Bowl of fruit (1 cup)
3	P/S/V	3–4 oz. roasted turkey breast 1 cup green beans ½ cup garlic mashed potato	3–4 oz. roasted turkey breast 1 cup green beans ½ cup garlic mashed potato
4	P/O	Chocolate raspberry shake: 20–25 g chocolate protein powder added to 10–12 oz. premade Crystal Light raspberry drink	Chocolate raspberry shake: 30–40 g chocolate protein powder added to 10–12 oz. premade Crystal Light raspberry drink
5	P/V/O	**Great Grilled Shrimp Kebabs** (See page 261.) 1 cup broccoli Salad with tomato, cucumber, and 1 tbsp. extra-virgin olive oil and vinegar or low-calorie, low-sugar dressing	**Great Grilled Shrimp Kebabs** (See page 261.) 1 cup broccoli Salad with tomato, cucumber, and 1 tbsp. extra-virgin olive oil and vinegar or low-calorie, low-sugar dressing
6	FF	1 serving sugar-free gelatin with 1 tbsp. Reddi-wip spray cream (not Cool Whip)	1 serving sugar-free gelatin with 1 tbsp. Reddi-wip spray cream (not Cool Whip)

Type Key
P = Protein S = Starch V = Vegetable O = Fat A = Fruit FF = Free Food

Notes

1. This sample food plan shows five meals and a sixth free-food meal. If you consume only four meals, you may skip meal 2 or 4. If you skip meal 2, you may have your fruit in meal 1 instead of a starch.

2. At meal 1, have a protein with a starch or fruit, not both. If you have a starch at meal 1, then you may have a fruit without a protein at meal 2. If you have a fruit with your protein at meal 1, then have just a protein at meal 2.

3. If you would like to substitute a different food at any particular meal, you must follow the type listed next to that meal and substitute the same type of food from your substitution list.

Your Notes

_____

_____

_____

_____

_____

_____

_____

_____

_____

_____

_____

_____

Maintenance Cycle Meal Plan H: High-Carb Day

MEAL	TYPE	WOMEN	MEN
1	P/S or A	**Wendy's Crepe** (See page 116.)	**Wendy's Crepe** (See page 116.)
2	P or A	1 apple	Bowl of fruit, 1 cup
3	P/S/V	3–4 oz. take-out Chinese lemon chicken 1 cup broccoli ½ cup rice	6 oz. take-out Chinese lemon chicken 1 cup broccoli 1 cup rice
4	P/O	**Mocha Protein Shake** (See page 90.)	**Mocha Protein Shake** (See page 90.)
5	P/S/V	4–6 oz. filet mignon 1 cup asparagus ½ baked potato	8 oz. filet mignon 1 cup asparagus 1 baked potato
6	FF	1 serving sugar-free gelatin with 1 tbsp. Reddi-wip spray cream (not Cool Whip)	1 serving sugar-free Gelatin with 1 tbsp. Reddi-wip spray cream (not Cool Whip)

Type Key

P = Protein S = Starch V = Vegetable O = Fat A = Fruit FF = Free Food

Notes

1. This sample food plan shows five meals and a sixth free-food meal. If you consume only four meals, you may skip meal 2 or 4. If you skip meal 2, you may have your fruit in meal 1 instead of a starch.

2. At meal 1, have a protein with a starch or fruit, not both. If you have a starch at meal 1, then you may have a fruit without a protein at meal 2. If you have a fruit with your protein at meal 1, then have just a protein at meal 2.

3. If you would like to substitute a different food at any particular meal, you must follow the type listed next to that meal and substitute the same type of food from your substitution list.

Your Notes

_____

_____

_____

_____

_____

_____

_____

_____

_____

_____

_____

_____

"I Didn't Just Lose Weight; I Gained the Body of My Dreams!"

Scott Tate

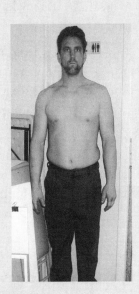 

I was a high school athlete, but after graduating, it seemed as if I was working more hours with little time to work out. If I did go back to work out, it seemed it took all my free time because I spent hours in the gym. I never had any idea about eating right, and I must confess, I always thought dieting meant eating salads and fruits. Not for me!

After taking Wendy's program, everything changed for me. I was never taught how food affects my body and that I could actually work out less but see more results by simply applying food to my exercise plan. I went from size 38 pants to size 32 and have six-pack abs. Wow, thanks Wendy!

> *I have followed Wendy's plan for three years now, and after my initial fat loss and muscle gain, I have maintained—and I believe even improved— my physique. As a result, I now have the opportunity for lifelong good health. I highly recommend this program to anyone and everyone. I feel great! Not only did Wendy help me drop the fat, but she also transformed my body.*

Wendy's "Mmm Good" Favorite Recipes for the Maintenance Cycle

When you begin the Maintenance Cycle, you can have fruit each morning on *any* day. Be advised, however, that you shouldn't eat fruit if you have diabetes.

Ham and Egg Hash

Use planners B and D

> 1 small potato, cubed (or use frozen breakfast
> potatoes from grocery freezer section)
>
> Salt and pepper to taste
>
> 1 whole egg plus 3 egg whites (for women), or 1
> whole egg plus 5 egg whites (for men), or have
> only egg whites or egg substitute, if desired
>
> 1 to 2 ounces cubed ham (deli ham sliced thick and
> cut into cubes works well)
>
> 1 to 2 ounces cheese, if desired

Spray skillet with nonstick cooking spray, and place over medium heat. Sauté potatoes until tender, seasoning with ground pepper and light salt. Beat eggs, and add ham. Pour into skillet over potatoes, and let set. Flip once, and cook until done. When ready, remove from skillet, and sprinkle with cheese if desired.

1 serving

Nutritional Value
Protein: 17 grams / 25 grams
Fat: 3 grams
Carbs: 15 grams

Fruit Smoothie

Use planners B and D

> 8 to 10 ounces water or fruit juice combination (4 ounces water plus 6 ounces juice)
>
> 1 to 1½ scoops vanilla protein powder
>
> ½ cup berries, any kind (I like frozen strawberries or blueberries)
>
> 4 to 5 ice cubes (fewer for thinner consistency, more for thicker shake)

Pour water or water and juice combo in blender. Add protein powder and fruit. Blend until smooth. Begin adding ice while blending until desired thickness is achieved. Drink immediately, or put in freezer to thicken more.

1 serving

Nutritional Value
Protein: Varies according to
   the kind of protein powder
   used; check label for
   values
Fat: 0 grams
Carbs: 12 to 25 grams,
   depending whether juice
   is used

Tuna-Stuffed Tomato

Use planners B, C, D

4 to 6 ounces well-drained canned white tuna

1 tablespoon real mayonnaise

¼ teaspoon dried dillweed

1 medium beefsteak tomato

Salt and pepper to taste

Lettuce leaves

In a bowl, combine tuna, mayo, and dill. Mix well. Core the tomato and stuff with tuna mixture. Sprinkle with pepper and light salt, and serve over a bed of lettuce.

1 serving

Nutritional Value
Protein: 22 to 30 grams
Fat: 6 grams
Carbs: 4 grams

Horseradish Beef Spears

Use planners B and D

> Horseradish sauce (available in the condiment aisle)
> or mustard
>
> 3 to 4 ounces sliced deli roast beef (great with
> turkey deli meat as well)
>
> 4 to 5 spears precooked asparagus (steaming in
> microwave for 1 minute is the quickest)

Spread horseradish sauce or mustard on beef, and wrap meat around each asparagus spear.

Avoiding mayo keeps the fat continent lower. I also like this with turkey breast, and it is a favorite traveling meal of mine. Yummy! This is a great snack or meal to take in the car.

1 serving

Nutritional Value
Protein: 25 to 35 grams
Fat: 6 grams
Carbs: 4 grams

Grilled Rosemary Balsamic Salmon

Use planners B, C, D

> 4 medium salmon fillets, ½" to 1" thick
>
> 2 teaspoons chopped fresh rosemary
>
> Salt and pepper to taste

Marinade

> ½ cup balsamic vinegar
>
> 1 tablespoon extra-virgin olive oil
>
> Juice from ½ lemon

Make the marinade by combining in a bowl the vinegar, olive oil, and lemon juice. Place salmon in a shallow container, and pour marinade over. Refrigerate 20 minutes to 1 hour. Pour marinade over salmon, and top with rosemary, light salt, and pepper. Grill over medium to hot heat until fish flakes, about 5 minutes for every ½-inch thickness of fish.

I like mine served over fresh baby spinach with additional balsamic vinegar poured on top.

4 servings

Nutritional Value
Protein: 25 grams
Fat: 12 grams (3 grams
   saturated fat, the rest
   healthful fats)
Carbs: 1 gram

PART 3

Living Forever Fit

9

Forever Fit

Restarting the Cycle

Welcome to forever! I mean that literally. *Crack the Fat-Loss Code* gives you a program you can follow for the rest of your life. I should know; I've been living it for over two decades now. Many of my clients have lived it for nearly as long—and now work side by side with me, helping others discover the joys of macro-patterning and sending your body to the "fat store" for energy needs.

I've designed this program as a lifestyle first and a diet second. It is full of convenience, realistic expectations, and even built-in cheat days. There are literally *no* forbidden foods, because that is simply not realistic. You can live on this plan forever, and here's how.

If, after two weeks on your maintenance cycle, you are interested in going back and restarting the cycle, keep in mind that you don't have to start from scratch or reinvent the wheel. The hard part is done. You've already learned to crack the fat-loss code, and now it's no longer necessary—or recommended—to go back and carb deplete.

Code Cracker

I've designed this program as a lifestyle first, a diet second.

Simply use four carb-down (C) days in a row—kind of like a "carb-deplete light"—and then restart your plan. Weeks 2 to 4 become weeks 10 to 13, weeks 5 to 6 become weeks 14 to 15, and weeks 7 to 8 become weeks 15 to 16. All the same meal plans, rules, and substitution lists apply. You just have to stay true to your program, your goals, and most importantly, yourself.

Remember, you already have the skills, knowledge, and practice you need to make this plan work—forever! The rest is up to you.

Code Cracker

Crack the Fat-Loss Code offers a program you can follow for the rest of your life. I should know; I've been living it for over two decades now.

Never Say *Diet*: Always Say *Lifestyle*

Never forget that this is a lifestyle, not a diet. The previous chapters gave you the keys to a new life, one you can drive off into the sunset and beyond. Diets give you temporary relief from a problem they don't thoroughly address, but *Crack the Fat-Loss Code* gives you a lifestyle you can follow—simply, easily, and comfortably—forever.

But knowledge can take you only so far; applying the knowledge is what turns a diet into a lifestyle. By now you should have had much success on your program. Don't stop there! Roll that success over into lifelong habits that truly allow you to achieve lifelong happiness.

Please don't stop with these eight weeks. You've come too far to stop now. Yes, you had to learn some new rules. Sure, you had to follow a food plan. Certainly, there were menus, options, choices, and even a few demands along the way. But all of that was to get you to this point: the point where you can take these tools and apply them to real life.

Code Cracker

You can't go forever without eating in a restaurant, attending a party, having a toast, or enjoying a slice of birthday cake.

Real life doesn't happen on a diet; real life happens when you come to terms with what works for you and create a lifestyle of good eating and exercise habits. You can't go forever without eating in a restaurant, attending a party, having a toast, or enjoying a slice of birthday cake. Life happens. But that doesn't mean we have to abandon a program or, even worse, abandon life.

This program was created by real people for real people. Your results are my results; my results are yours. You have gained invaluable knowledge over the course of this program— knowledge that has the power to change lives. I know because I've seen it happen firsthand.

This chapter is all about hope: hope for the future, hope for the courage to sustain the program, and hope for the possibility that exists just beyond the pages of this book. Don't skip this chapter to get to the food plan. Instead, use it to make the food plan even more valuable as one part of your brand-new lifestyle, the ForeverFit lifestyle.

Code Cracker

Diets give you temporary relief from a problem they don't thoroughly address, but Crack the Fat-Loss Code gives you a lifestyle you can follow—simply, easily, and comfortably—forever.

Ten Keys to Fat-Loss Success

Success doesn't happen overnight. Sometimes it doesn't even happen in eight weeks. Life is for the living, for the making of mistakes and learning from them. Here are my ten keys to fat-loss success. Read and apply them, so you can attain success and stick to your program forever.

1. **Set realistic short-term goals.** The best way to think of these is as "mini goals." When I was actively training in road racing, I didn't start out running a marathon. I started with lower-mileage races, and in each race, I would try to better my time and better my distance until I was running a competitive marathon. There is no way to reach a huge long-term goal without a few mini goals along the way. What are your mini goals?

2. **Short-term goals should lead you to long-term goals.** Allow for occasional setbacks along the way, but regard them as learning experiences. That's the beauty of short-term, or mini, goals. You can make a few missteps along the way and still reach your ultimate goal, as long as you simply learn from your misstep and get back on track.

3. **Set a training schedule and stick to it.** It helps to have a contract with yourself. How formal you make this "contract" is

up to you. Some clients put the schedule in writing; others tack it to their fridge or keep a sticky note in their wallets. Some keep it in their heads. But all do one thing in common: stick to it.

4. **Listen to your body.** If I've taught you one thing in this book, it's to listen to your body. We talked about not eating too much (stuffing) and not eating too little (starving). Your body sends you signals when it's too full or too empty; listening to them is one way to stay in balance. Your exercise should be the same. Fatigue is a sign to take a break, and it's OK to do so. The old adage of "no pain, no gain" has gone by the wayside.

5. **Constantly challenge yourself.** Life is meant to be a challenge. We strive to meet challenges and move beyond them. If we don't learn, we can't grow. Success is like a muscle; it doesn't grow if it isn't stretched. How far can you stretch today?

6. **Devise your own personal definition of success.** This is *so* important. Often we compare ourselves to others, doing ourselves a disservice in the process. But let's face it: not all of us were meant to be six-foot-two and wear a size 4. Be more than just content with who you are and what you've done; be happy about it. Find success on your own terms, not somebody else's.

7. **Believe in yourself.** You are special; you are worthy. And the one person in control of your own personal destiny is you. Listen to positive people, listen to your trainer, your nutritionist, your mentors, family, and friends, but believe in yourself. At the end of the day, you can be either your own worst enemy or your very best friend. The choice is up to you.

8. **Surround yourself with a team of positive people who motivate you to succeed.** We all need others to make it in this world, whether it's at the dinner table or in the gym. Smart people surround themselves with other smart people; successful people do the same thing. Being around negative doubters who question your every move and complain "you'll never do that" is one sure way to prove them right!

9. **Make planning the most important part of your program.** Making a plan is your first step toward ensuring your success. It really *is* the most important part of your program,

because without a plan, there would be no program. This book started as a plan; each chapter had its own plan. Every word, sentence, paragraph, and page was a plan within a plan. That is how great feats are accomplished; that is how success is achieved.

10. **Realize that "life" happens, enjoy each day, and know that life is magnificent.** You are no longer a prisoner of your body. Now you can realize that your body does not run your life; you do. Live life again. Experience it for all the joy it has to offer. Being healthy, fit, and in control of your eating decisions frees you up to enjoy life to the fullest. Don't waste another minute dwelling on your appearance; be proud of who you are, and live life now!

||||||||||| FAT-LOSS FACT |||||||||||

Smart people surround themselves with other smart people; successful people do the same thing. Being around negative doubters who question your every move and complain "you'll never do that" is one sure way to prove them right.

The Future Starts Now

Congratulations on completing your own personal journey to crack the fat-loss code. I encourage you to take the knowledge you've gained here and apply it to every facet of your life from this day forward.

Don't waste another day complaining about fad diets or fat-free snacks or other useless ventures. You've put all that behind you now, because you know the secret to cracking the fat-loss code is manipulating your energy stores through macro-patterning.

"Wendy Helped Me Get off the Yo-Yo Roller-Coaster"

Tony Clifford

I was always an active kid. I played Pop Warner football and soccer and continued the tradition all the way through high school with football and track. Later I played football in college and also competed in Olympic weight lifting and attained a ranking of seventy-fifth in the nation. After college, I continued to work out and lift weights three days a week. I was very in tune to what was going into my body, my workouts, and beginning my career in the food industry.

All of that changed when I left California and took on more for a career. While doing that, I lost focus on structure, working out, and my eating. I started gaining weight because I wasn't doing

(continued)

any workout activity. I was no longer involved in sports, not even on a recreational level. Thanks to my new job, different patterns took over my life: eating late, excessive drinking, etc. For the next ten years, I worked, gained weight, and progressively got more out of shape.

After some life-changing events occurred in my life, in January of this year I had an awakening and attempted to get a regimen back in my daily life, working out and eating better. I had minimal success, losing and gaining back the same five pounds on a yo-yo roller-coaster. Then I was introduced to Wendy's eight-week Nutrition Boot Camp, and I found a system that worked for me.

Within two weeks, I saw substantial loss in weight and increase in energy. I stayed on the program, went to the classes, and by trimming back on daily intake and following the meal plans, I was able to continue to drop weight. The eight-week program gave me a great structure to lose and maintain the weight loss. I was able to continue after the eight weeks with the eating and workout concepts, and I'm still seeing results. I haven't reached my goal as of yet. However, it's a lot easier to know that the weight is still coming off, and it gives me the sense that I have the possibility to reach my goals soon.

Life is imperfect; so are we. Don't worry if you get off plan or slide back into old habits. There is no deadline for success. Just get back on the program and stay there. You have the tools; it's up to you to use them for the rest of your life.

Don't let appearance rule your life. Fat loss is just one aspect of who you are. It may have dominated your past eight weeks, but let that be a means to an end. By taking these eight weeks now, you have given yourself a bright and unlimited future. You should feel as if you've been unshackled from your scale. How liberating! While fat will always be a part of our lives, it shouldn't rule our lives.

Now that you have the understanding to crack the fat-loss code—you know what it takes to eat right, eat often, eat less, and even eat better—eating doesn't have to be the main event. Let it become background noise, and quit obsessing about every bite you put into your mouth. This plan is simple, easy, satisfying, and repeatable. If you're like me—if you're like most men and women in this country—you have obsessed about excess fat for far too long. You know how they say we should think *outside of the box*? Well, now it's time to live your life *outside of the fridge*. Life is out there, waiting just past your kitchen walls.

Take the first step, and let your future start now!

FAT-LOSS FACT

Fat loss is just one aspect of who you are. It may have dominated your past eight weeks, but let that be a means to an end. By taking these eight weeks now, you have given yourself a bright and unlimited future.

10

Sample Meal Plans

Your Eight-Week Planner

The following pages will guide you through a sample week of each of the four cycles of the plan for cracking the fat-loss code. They include the Carb-Deplete, Macro-Patterning, Accelerated Fat-Loss, and Maintenance Cycles.

Eight-Week Meal Plans at a Glance

To help you keep track of what to eat and when, here are the eight-week meal plans at a glance.

Weeks 1–3

Week 1 Meal Plan

| Planner A | Mon | Tues | Wed | Thurs | Fri | Sat | Sun |
	Day 1	Day 2	Day 3	Day 4	Day 5	Day 6	Day 7
Carb-Deplete Cycle	Carbs: Under 20 g	Carbs: Under 20 g	Carbs: Under 20 g	Carbs: Under 20 g	Carbs: Under 20 g	Carbs: Under 20 g	Carbs: Under 20 g

Week 2 Meal Plan

Planners B, C, D	Mon Day 8	Tues Day 9	Wed Day 10	Thurs Day 11	Fri Day 12	Sat Day 13	Sun Day 14
Cycle Day	C	C	B	B	C	D	B
Starch Amount	1 time before 3:00 P.M.	1 time before 3:00 P.M.	2 times before 3:00 P.M.	2 times before 3:00 P.M.	1 time before 3:00 P.M.	Last 2 meals	2 times before 3:00 P.M.

Week 3 Meal Plan

Planners B, C, D	Mon Day 15	Tues Day 16	Wed Day 17	Thurs Day 18	Fri Day 19	Sat Day 20	Sun Day 21
Cycle Day	B	C	D	B	C	D	B
Starch Amount	2 times before 3:00 P.M.	1 time before 3:00 P.M.	Last 2 meals	2 times before 3:00 P.M.	1 time before 3:00 P.M.	Last 2 meals	2 times before 3:00 P.M.

Weeks 4–6

Week 4 Meal Plan

Planners B, C, D	Mon Day 22	Tues Day 23	Wed Day 24	Thurs Day 25	Fri Day 26	Sat Day 27	Sun Day 28
Cycle Day	B	C	D	B	C	D	B
Starch Amount	2 times before 3:00 P.M.	1 time before 3:00 P.M.	Last 2 meals	2 times before 3:00 P.M.	1 time before 3:00 P.M.	Last 2 meals	2 times before 3:00 P.M.

Week 5 Meal Plan

Planners B, C, D	Mon Day 29	Tues Day 30	Wed Day 31	Thurs Day 32	Fri Day 33	Sat Day 34	Sun Day 35
Cycle Day	C	C	D	B	C	D	B
Starch Amount	1 time before 3:00 P.M.	1 time before 3:00 P.M.	Last 2 meals	2 times before 3:00 P.M.	1 time before 3:00 P.M.	Last 2 meals	2 times before 3:00 P.M.

Week 6 Meal Plan

Planners B, C, D	Mon Day 36	Tues Day 37	Wed Day 38	Thurs Day 39	Fri Day 40	Sat Day 41	Sun Day 42
Cycle Day	C	C	D	B	C	D	B
Starch Amount	1 time before 3:00 P.M.	1 time before 3:00 P.M.	Last 2 meals	2 times before 3:00 P.M.	1 time before 3:00 P.M.	Last 2 meals	2 times before 3:00 P.M.

Weeks 7–8

Weeks 7–8 Meal Plan

Planners B, CH, H	Mon	Tues	Wed	Thurs	Fri	Sat	Sun
Maintenance	B	B	B	B	B	CH	H

Cycle 1: Carb-Deplete Cycle

Information without action isn't any way to crack the fat-loss code, so now it's time to use all that information and put it into action. To get you off to a great—and quick—start, the following pages include the sample meal plans for the entire week of the Carb-Deplete Cycle.

Carb-Deplete Cycle Meal Plan A: Monday

MEAL	TYPE	WOMEN	MEN
1	P/O	**Wendy's Egg Cheeseburger** (See page 87.)	**Wendy's Egg Cheeseburger** (See page 87.)
2	P/O	½ cup cottage cheese (full-fat brand so carbs are reduced)	Vanilla shake: 30–40 g vanilla protein powder blended with 10–12 oz. water and ice for desired thickness
3	P/V/O	Chicken Caesar salad: 3–4 oz. chicken on large lettuce and cucumber salad with 1 tbsp. extra-virgin olive oil and vinegar (watch carb count)	Chicken Caesar salad: 6–8 oz. chicken on large lettuce and cucumber salad with 1 tbsp. extra-virgin olive oil and vinegar (watch carb count)
4	P/O	**Orange Dream Protein Shake** (See page 89.)	**Orange Dream Protein Shake** (See page 89.)
5	P/V/O	4–6 oz. grilled salmon fillet 1 cup broccoli Lettuce and cucumber salad with 1 tbsp. extra-virgin olive oil and vinegar or full-fat dressing (watch carb count)	6–8 oz. grilled salmon fillet 1 cup broccoli Lettuce and cucumber salad with 1 tbsp. extra-virgin olive oil and vinegar or full-fat dressing (watch carb count)
6	P/O	Scrambled eggs: 1 whole egg with 2–3 egg whites, scrambled and topped with cheese	Scrambled eggs: 1 whole egg with 4–5 egg whites, scrambled and topped with cheese

Type Key

P = Protein   V = Vegetable   O = Fat

Notes

1. This sample food plan shows six meals. If you consume only four meals, you may skip meal 2 or 4 and meal 6, for a total of four meals that day.

2. If you consume only five meals, then you may skip meal 2 or 4 or 6, for a total of five meals.

3. If you would like to substitute a different food at any particular meal, you must follow the type listed next to that meal and substitute the same type of food from your substitution list.

Your Notes

_____

_____

_____

_____

_____

_____

_____

_____

_____

_____

_____

_____

_____

_____

_____

Carb-Deplete Cycle Meal Plan A: Tuesday

MEAL	TYPE	WOMEN	MEN
1	P/O	**Mushroom and Spinach Omelet** (See page 88.)	**Mushroom and Spinach Omelet** (See page 88.)
2	P/O	3 oz. turkey roll-up with cheese	**Orange Dream Protein Shake** (See page 89.)
3	P/V/O	Chicken Caesar salad: 3–4 oz. chicken on large lettuce and cucumber salad with 1 tbsp. extra-virgin olive oil and vinegar (watch carb count)	Chicken Caesar salad: 6–8 oz. chicken on large lettuce and cucumber salad with 1 tbsp. extra-virgin olive oil and vinegar (watch carb count)
4	P/O	**Mocha Protein Shake** (See page 90.)	**Mocha Protein Shake** (See page 90.)
5	P/V/O	4 oz. top sirloin steak with mushrooms 1 cup broccoli Lettuce and cucumber salad with 1 tbsp. extra-virgin olive oil and vinegar or full-fat dressing (watch carb count)	6–8 oz. T-bone steak with mushrooms 1 cup broccoli Lettuce and cucumber salad with 1 tbsp. extra-virgin olive oil and vinegar or full-fat dressing (watch carb count)
6	P/O	½ cup cottage cheese (full-fat brand so carbs are reduced)	5 oz. turkey roll-up with cheese

Type Key
P = Protein   V = Vegetable   O = Fat

Notes

1. This sample food plan shows six meals. If you consume only four meals, you may skip meal 2 or 4 and meal 6, for a total of four meals that day.

2. If you consume only five meals, then you may skip meal 2 or 4 or 6, for a total of five meals.

3. If you would like to substitute a different food at any particular meal, you must follow the type listed next to that meal and substitute the same type of food from your substitution list.

Your Notes

_____

_____

_____

_____

_____

_____

_____

_____

_____

_____

_____

_____

_____

Carb-Deplete Cycle Meal Plan A: Wednesday

MEAL	TYPE	WOMEN	MEN
1	P/O	**Wendy's Egg Cheeseburger** (See page 87.)	**Wendy's Egg Cheeseburger** (See page 87.)
2	P/O	½ cup cottage cheese (full-fat brand so carbs are reduced)	Vanilla shake: 30–40 g vanilla protein powder blended with 10–12 oz. water and ice for desired thickness
3	P/V/O	**Tasty Turkey Taco Salad** (See page 254.)	**Tasty Turkey Taco Salad** (See page 254.)
4	P/O	**Orange Dream Protein Shake** (See page 89.)	**Orange Dream Protein Shake** (See page 89.)
5	P/V/O	4–6 oz. grilled Cajun chicken (grilled lightly and coated with cayenne pepper) 1 cup broccoli Lettuce and cucumber salad with 1 tbsp. extra-virgin olive oil and vinegar or full-fat dressing (watch carb count)	6–8 oz. grilled Cajun chicken (grilled lightly and coated with cayenne pepper) 1 cup broccoli Lettuce and cucumber salad with 1 tbsp. extra-virgin olive oil and vinegar or full-fat dressing (watch carb count)
6	P/O	Chocolate raspberry shake: 20–25 g chocolate protein powder added to 10–12 oz. premade Crystal Light raspberry drink	8 oz. cottage cheese (full-fat brand so carbs are reduced)

Type Key

P = Protein   V = Vegetable   O = Fat

Notes

1. This sample food plan shows six meals. If you consume only four meals, you may skip meal 2 or 4 and meal 6, for a total of four meals that day.

2. If you consume only five meals, then you may skip meal 2 or 4 or 6, for a total of five meals.

3. If you would like to substitute a different food at any particular meal, you must follow the type listed next to that meal and substitute the same type of food from your substitution list.

Your Notes

_____

_____

_____

_____

_____

_____

_____

_____

_____

_____

_____

_____

_____

Carb-Deplete Cycle Meal Plan A: Thursday

MEAL	TYPE	WOMEN	MEN
1	P/O	**Mushroom and Spinach Omelet** (See page 88.)	**Mushroom and Spinach Omelet** (See page 88.)
2	P/O	3 oz. turkey roll-up with cheese	Vanilla shake: 30–40 g vanilla protein powder blended with 10–12 oz. water and ice for desired thickness
3	P/V/O	Chicken Caesar salad: 3–4 oz. chicken on large lettuce and cucumber salad with 1 tbsp. extra-virgin olive oil and vinegar (watch carb count)	Chicken Caesar salad: 6–8 oz. chicken on large lettuce and cucumber salad with 1 tbsp. extra-virgin olive oil and vinegar (watch carb count)
4	P/O	**Orange Dream Protein Shake** (See page 89.)	5 oz. turkey roll-up with cheese
5	P/V/O	4–6 oz. grilled salmon 1 cup broccoli Lettuce and cucumber salad with 1 tbsp. extra-virgin olive oil and vinegar or full-fat dressing (watch carb count)	6–8 oz. grilled salmon 1 cup broccoli Lettuce and cucumber salad with 1 tbsp. extra-virgin olive oil and vinegar or full-fat dressing (watch carb count)
6	P/O	½ cup cottage cheese (full-fat brand so carbs are reduced)	**Orange Dream Protein Shake** (See page 89.)
Type Key			
P = Protein V = Vegetable O = Fat			

Notes

1. This sample food plan shows six meals. If you consume only four meals, you may skip meal 2 or 4 and meal 6, for a total of four meals that day.

2. If you consume only five meals, then you may skip meal 2 or 4 or 6, for a total of five meals.

3. If you would like to substitute a different food at any particular meal, you must follow the type listed next to that meal and substitute the same type of food from your substitution list.

Your Notes

_____

_____

_____

_____

_____

_____

_____

_____

_____

_____

_____

_____

_____

Carb-Deplete Cycle Meal Plan A: Friday

MEAL	TYPE	WOMEN	MEN
1	P/O	**Mushroom and Spinach Omelet** (See page 88.)	**Mushroom and Spinach Omelet** (See page 88.)
2	P/O	½ cup cottage cheese (full-fat brand so carbs are reduced)	**Orange Dream Protein Shake** (See page 89.)
3	P/V/O	3–4 oz. tuna on large lettuce and cucumber salad with 1 tbsp. real mayonnaise	6–8 oz. tuna on large lettuce and cucumber salad with 1 tbsp. real mayonnaise
4	P/O	**Mocha Protein Shake** (See page 90.)	**Mocha Protein Shake** (See page 90.)
5	P/V/O	4–6 oz. roasted turkey breast 1 cup broccoli Lettuce and cucumber salad with 1 tbsp. extra-virgin olive oil and vinegar or full-fat dressing (watch carb count)	6–8 oz. roasted turkey breast 1 cup broccoli Lettuce and cucumber salad with 1 tbsp. extra-virgin olive oil and vinegar or full-fat dressing (watch carb count)
6	P/O	Scrambled eggs: 1 whole egg plus 2–3 egg whites, scrambled and topped with cheese	Scrambled eggs: 1 whole egg plus 4–5 egg whites, scrambled and topped with cheese

Type Key

P = Protein   V = Vegetable   O = Fat

Notes

1. This sample food plan shows six meals. If you consume only four meals, you may skip meal 2 or 4 and meal 6, for a total of four meals that day.

2. If you consume only five meals, then you may skip meal 2 or 4 or 6, for a total of five meals.

3. If you would like to substitute a different food at any particular meal, you must follow the type listed next to that meal and substitute the same type of food from your substitution list.

Your Notes

_____

_____

_____

_____

_____

_____

_____

_____

_____

_____

_____

_____

_____

Carb-Deplete Cycle Meal Plan A: Saturday

MEAL	TYPE	WOMEN	MEN
1	P/O	**Mocha Protein Shake** (See page 90.)	**Mocha Protein Shake** (See page 90.)
2	P/O	3 oz. turkey roll-up with cheese	5 oz. turkey roll-up with cheese
3	P/V/O	Chicken Caesar salad: 3–4 oz. chicken on large lettuce and cucumber salad with 1 tbsp. extra-virgin olive oil and vinegar (watch carb count)	Chicken Caesar salad: 6–8 oz. chicken on large lettuce and cucumber salad with 1 tbsp. extra-virgin olive oil and vinegar (watch carb count)
4	P/O	**Orange Dream Protein Shake** (See page 89.)	**Orange Dream Protein Shake** (See page 89.)
5	P/V/O	4–6 oz. filet mignon with mushrooms 1 cup broccoli Lettuce and cucumber salad with 1 tbsp. extra-virgin olive oil and vinegar or full-fat dressing (watch carb count)	6–8 oz. filet mignon with mushrooms 1 cup broccoli Lettuce and cucumber salad with 1 tbsp. extra-virgin olive oil and vinegar or full-fat dressing (watch carb count)
6	P/O	½ cup cottage cheese (full-fat brand so carbs are reduced)	Vanilla shake: 30–40 g vanilla protein powder blended with 10–12 oz. water and ice for desired thickness

Type Key
P = Protein   V = Vegetable   O = Fat

Notes

1. This sample food plan shows six meals. If you consume only four meals, you may skip meal 2 or 4 and meal 6, for a total of four meals that day.

2. If you consume only five meals, then you may skip meal 2 or 4 or 6, for a total of five meals.

3. If you would like to substitute a different food at any particular meal, you must follow the type listed next to that meal and substitute the same type of food from your substitution list.

Your Notes

_____

_____

_____

_____

_____

_____

_____

_____

_____

_____

_____

_____

Carb-Deplete Cycle Meal Plan A: Sunday

MEAL	TYPE	WOMEN	MEN
1	P/O	**Wendy's Egg Cheeseburger** (See page 87.)	**Wendy's Egg Cheeseburger** (See page 87.)
2	P/O	½ cup cottage cheese (full-fat brand so carbs are reduced)	**Orange Dream Protein Shake** (See page 89.)
3	P/V/O	Chef salad: 3–4 oz. turkey breast or chicken, 2 oz. cheese, 1 hard-boiled egg, lettuce, and cucumber, with 1 tbsp. extra-virgin olive oil and vinegar (watch carb count)	Chef salad: 6 oz. turkey breast or chicken, 2 oz. cheese, 1 hard-boiled egg, lettuce, and cucumber, with 1 tbsp. extra-virgin olive oil and vinegar (watch carb count)
4	P/O	**Mocha Protein Shake** (See page 90.)	**Mocha Protein Shake** (See page 90.)
5	P/V/O	4–6 oz. grilled chicken 1 cup broccoli Lettuce and cucumber salad with 1 tbsp. extra-virgin olive oil and vinegar or full-fat dressing (watch carb count)	6–8 oz. grilled chicken 1 cup broccoli Lettuce and cucumber salad with 1 tbsp. extra-virgin olive oil and vinegar or full-fat dressing (watch carb count)
6	P/O	Chocolate raspberry shake: 20–25 g chocolate protein powder added to 10–12 oz. premade Crystal Light raspberry drink	Chocolate raspberry shake: 30–40 g chocolate protein powder added to 10–12 oz. premade Crystal Light raspberry drink

Type Key

P = Protein   V = Vegetable   O = Fat

Notes

1. This sample food plan shows six meals. If you consume only four meals, you may skip meal 2 or 4 and meal 6, for a total of four meals that day.

2. If you consume only five meals, then you may skip meal 2 or 4 or 6, for a total of five meals.

3. If you would like to substitute a different food at any particular meal, you must follow the type listed next to that meal and substitute the same type of food from your substitution list.

Your Notes

_____

_____

_____

_____

_____

_____

_____

_____

Cycle 2: Macro-Patterning Cycle

On the following pages, you will find an example of one week of the Macro-Patterning Cycle as a guide for completing a macro-patterning week. This will show you how easy it is to make the transition from the first cycle to the second. After viewing the sample meal plans, you'll have a great idea of how much food—and what a wide variety of food—you can and should eat during this all-important cycle.

Macro-Patterning Cycle Meal Planner B:
Monday, Baseline Day

MEAL	TYPE	WOMEN	MEN
1	P/S	**Power Oats** (See page 117.)	**Power Oats** (See page 117.)
2	P/O	½ cup cottage cheese	Vanilla shake: 30–40 g vanilla protein powder blended with 10–12 oz. water and ice for desired thickness
3	P/S/V	3–4 oz. roasted turkey breast 1 cup green beans ½ cup garlic mashed potato	3–4 oz. roasted turkey breast 1 cup green beans ½ cup garlic mashed potato
4	P/O	Chocolate raspberry shake: 20–25 g chocolate protein powder added to 10–12 oz. premade Crystal Light raspberry drink	Chocolate raspberry shake: 30–40 g chocolate protein powder added to 10–12 oz. premade Crystal Light raspberry drink
5	P/V/O	**Great Grilled Shrimp Kebabs** (See page 261.) 1 cup broccoli Salad with tomato, cucumber, and 1 tbsp. extra-virgin olive oil and vinegar or low-calorie, low-sugar dressing	**Great Grilled Shrimp Kebabs** (See page 261.) 1 cup broccoli Salad with tomato, cucumber, and 1 tbsp. extra-virgin olive oil and vinegar or low-calorie, low-sugar dressing
6	FF	1 serving sugar-free gelatin with 1 tbsp. Reddi-wip spray cream (not Cool Whip)	1 serving sugar-free gelatin with 1 tbsp. Reddi-wip spray cream (not Cool Whip)

Type Key

P = Protein   S = Starch   V = Vegetable   O = Fat   FF = Free Food

Notes

1. This sample food plan shows five meals and a sixth free-food meal. If you consume only four meals, you may skip meal 2 or 4, for a total of four meals that day.

2. Make sure to consume one starch in two different meals before 3:00 P.M.

3. If you would like to substitute a different food at any particular meal, you must follow the type listed next to that meal and substitute the same type of food from your substitution list.

Your Notes

_____

_____

_____

_____

_____

_____

_____

_____

_____

_____

_____

_____

_____

_____

Macro-Patterning Cycle Meal Planner C:
Tuesday, Carb-Down Day

MEAL	TYPE	WOMEN	MEN
1	P/S	**Wendy's Crepe** (See page 116.)	**Wendy's Crepe** (See page 116.)
2	P/O	½ cup cottage cheese	Vanilla shake: 30–40 g vanilla protein powder blended with 10–12 oz. water and ice for desired thickness
3	P/V	3–4 oz. grilled chicken Lettuce wraps with cabbage, cucumber, onion, tomato, and salsa	6 oz. grilled chicken Lettuce wraps with cabbage, cucumber, onion, tomato, and salsa
4	P/O	Chocolate raspberry shake: 20–25 g chocolate protein powder added to 10–12 oz. premade Crystal Light raspberry drink	Chocolate raspberry shake: 30–40 g chocolate protein powder added to 10–12 oz. premade Crystal Light raspberry drink
5	P/V/O	4–6 oz. broiled salmon or halibut 1 cup asparagus Salad with tomato, cucumber, and 1 tbsp. extra-virgin olive oil and vinegar or low-calorie, low-sugar dressing	8 oz. broiled salmon or halibut 1 cup asparagus Salad with tomato, cucumber, and 1 tbsp. extra-virgin olive oil and vinegar or low-calorie, low-sugar dressing
6	P	Crispy lettuce wrap: 3–4 oz. turkey breast and 1–2 slices cheese, rolled in large Bibb lettuce leaf with mustard or light mayonnaise	**Orange Dream Protein Shake** (See page 89.)

Type Key
P = Protein   S = Starch   V = Vegetable   O = Fat

Notes

1. This sample food plan shows six meals. If you consume only four meals, you may skip meal 2 or 4 and meal 6, for a total of four meals that day.

2. If you consume only five meals, then you may skip meal 2 or 4 or 6, for a total of five meals.

3. If you would like to substitute a different food at any particular meal, you must follow the type listed next to that meal and substitute the same type of food from your substitution list.

4. Make sure to eat one starch in one meal before 3:00 P.M.

Your Notes

_____

_____

_____

_____

_____

_____

_____

_____

_____

_____

_____

Macro-Patterning Cycle Meal Planner D:
Wednesday, Carb-Up Day (Nondiabetic)

MEAL	TYPE	WOMEN	MEN
1	P/S	Eggs on a bagel: 1 whole egg plus 2–3 egg whites, scrambled and served on ½ bagel	Eggs on a bagel: 1 whole egg plus 4–5 egg whites, scrambled and served on 1 bagel
2	P/O	½ cup cottage cheese	Chocolate raspberry shake: 30–40 g chocolate protein powder added to 10–12 oz. premade Crystal Light raspberry drink
3	P/V/O	Chicken Caesar salad: 3–4 oz. chicken on large lettuce and cucumber salad, with 1 tbsp. extra-virgin olive oil and vinegar (croutons OK)	Chicken Caesar salad: 6–8 oz. chicken on large lettuce and cucumber salad, with 1 tbsp. extra-virgin olive oil and vinegar (croutons OK)
4	SA or A	Chips and salsa (*Don't stuff*)	Chips and salsa (*Don't stuff*)
5	SA	Plate of pasta with 1 meatball and marinara sauce 1 small roll (*Don't stuff*)	Plate of pasta with 1 meatball and marinara sauce 1 roll (*Don't stuff*)

Type Key

P = Protein   S = Starch   V = Vegetable   O = Fat   A = Fruit

SA = Sweets and Alcohol

Notes

1. This sample food plan is for a nondiabetic carb-up day. If, after trying this plan, you feel lethargic or sickly, you may be carb-sensitive. In that case, the following diabetic carb-up plan may work better for you.

2. This sample food plan shows five meals. If you consume only four meals, you may skip meal 2, if you are currently doing cardio and weight training. If you are not doing cardio and weight training, only the last meal may be a carb-up meal.

3. If you are not exercising, have only one carb-up meal as the last meal of the day.

4. Wait until after day 21 to consume cakes, other sweet starches, and alcohol.

5. Don't overeat at your carb-up meal. Eat until you're satisfied, not stuffed.

6. If you would like to substitute a different food at any particular meal, you must follow the type listed next to that meal and substitute the same type of food from your substitution list.

Your Notes

_____

_____

_____

_____

_____

_____

_____

Macro-Patterning Cycle Meal Planner D:
Wednesday, Carb-Up Day (Diabetic)

MEAL	TYPE	WOMEN	MEN
1	P/S	Eggs on a bagel: 1 whole egg plus 2–3 egg whites, scrambled, served on ½ bagel	Eggs on a bagel: 1 whole egg plus 4–5 egg whites, scrambled, served on 1 bagel
2	P/O	½ cup cottage cheese	Chocolate raspberry shake: 30–40 g chocolate protein powder added to 10–12 oz. premade Crystal Light raspberry drink
3	P/SA	6-in. sub sandwich 1 small bag chips	6-in. sub sandwich 1 small bag chips
4	P/SA	Crispy lettuce wrap: 2–3 oz. turkey breast and cheese, rolled in large leaf lettuce 1 cup berries or ½ melon	Vanilla shake with berries or banana: 30–40 g vanilla protein powder blended with 10–12 oz. water, fruit, and ice for desired thickness
5	SA	Pasta with chicken and marinara sauce 1 roll (*Don't stuff*)	Pasta with chicken and marinara sauce 1 roll (*Don't stuff*)

Type Key

P = Protein   S = Starch   V = Vegetable   O = Fat   A = Fruit

SA = Sweets and Alcohol

Notes

1. This sample food plan is a carb-up day for a person with diabetes. The idea is to have small amounts of carbs through your day with protein. Individuals who are sensitive to carbs also may prefer using this plan.

2. This plan shows five meals. If you consume only four meals, you may skip meal #2.

3. Do not consume cakes, other sweet starches, or alcohol until after day 21.

4. Don't overeat at any meal. Eat until satisfied, not stuffed.

5. If you would like to substitute a different food at any particular meal, you must follow the type listed next to that meal and substitute the same type of food from your substitution list.

Your Notes

_____

_____

_____

_____

_____

_____

_____

_____

_____

Macro-Patterning Cycle Meal Planner B:
Thursday, Baseline Day

MEAL	TYPE	WOMEN	MEN
1	P/S	**Wendy's Crepe** (See page 116.)	**Wendy's Crepe** (See page 116.)
2	P/O	Crispy lettuce wrap: 2–3 oz. turkey breast and cheese rolled in large leaf lettuce	Vanilla shake with berries or banana: 30–40 g vanilla protein powder blended with 10–12 oz. water, fruit, and ice for desired thickness
3	P/S/V	3–4 oz. top sirloin steak with mushrooms 1 cup broccoli ½ baked potato with ½ tsp. butter	6–8 oz. top sirloin steak with mushrooms 1 cup broccoli ½ baked potato with ½ tsp. butter
4	P/O	Chocolate raspberry shake: 20–25 g chocolate protein powder added to 10–12 oz. premade Crystal Light raspberry drink	**Orange Dream Protein Shake** (See page 89.)
5	P/V/O	4–6 oz. grilled chicken 1 cup green beans Lettuce and cucumber salad with 1 tbsp. extra-virgin olive oil and vinegar or full-fat dressing (watch carb count)	6–8 oz. grilled chicken 1 cup green beans Lettuce and cucumber salad with 1 tbsp. extra-virgin olive oil and vinegar or full-fat dressing (watch carb count)
6	FF	1 serving sugar-free gelatin with 1 tbsp. Reddi-wip spray cream (not Cool Whip)	1 serving sugar-free gelatin with 1 tbsp. Reddi-wip spray cream (not Cool Whip)

Type Key
P = Protein   S = Starch   V = Vegetable   O = Fat   FF = Free Food

Notes

1. This sample food plan shows five meals and a sixth free-food meal. If you consume only four meals, you may skip meal 2 or 4, for a total of four meals that day.

2. Make sure to consume one starch in two different meals before 3:00 P.M.

3. If you would like to substitute a different food at any particular meal, you must follow the type listed next to that meal and substitute the same type of food from your substitution list.

Your Notes

_____

_____

_____

_____

_____

_____

_____

_____

_____

_____

_____

_____

_____

_____

Macro-Patterning Cycle Meal Planner C:
Friday, Carb-Down Day

MEAL	TYPE	WOMEN	MEN
1	P/O	**Mushroom and Spinach Omelet** (See page 88.)	**Mushroom and Spinach Omelet** (See page 88.)
2	P/O	½ cup cottage cheese	Vanilla shake with berries or banana: 30–40 g vanilla protein powder blended with 10–12 oz. water, fruit, and ice for desired thickness
3	P/S/V	3–4 oz. **Citrus Grilled Chicken** (See page 120.) 1 cup broccoli ½ small sweet potato	6–8 oz. **Citrus Grilled Chicken** (See page 120.) 1 cup broccoli 1 small sweet potato
4	P/O	**Mocha Protein Shake** (See page 90.)	**Mocha Protein Shake** (See page 90.)
5	P/V/O	4–6 oz. grilled salmon 1 cup asparagus Salad with tomato, cucumber, and 1 tbsp. extra-virgin olive oil and vinegar or low-calorie, low-sugar dressing	8 oz. grilled salmon 1 cup asparagus Salad with tomato, cucumber, 1 tbsp. extra-virgin olive oil and vinegar or low-calorie, low-sugar dressing
6	P	Chocolate raspberry shake: 20–25 g chocolate protein powder added to 10–12 oz. of premade Crystal Light raspberry drink	Chocolate raspberry shake: 30–40 g chocolate protein powder added to 10–12 oz. premade Crystal Light raspberry drink

Type Key
P = Protein   S = Starch   V = Vegetable   O = Fat

Notes

1. This sample food plan shows six meals. If you consume only four meals, you may skip meal 2 or 4 and meal 6, for a total of four meals that day.

2. If you consume only five meals, then you may skip meal 2 or 4 or 6, for a total of five meals.

3. If you would like to substitute a different food at any particular meal, you must follow the type listed next to that meal and substitute the same type of food from your substitution list.

4. Make sure to eat one starch in one meal before 3:00 P.M.

Your Notes

_____

_____

_____

_____

_____

_____

_____

_____

_____

_____

Macro-Patterning Cycle Meal Planner D:
Saturday, Carb-Up Day (Nondiabetic)

MEAL	TYPE	WOMEN	MEN
1	P/S	Eggs on a bagel: 1 whole egg plus 2-3 egg whites, scrambled, served on ½ bagel	Eggs on a bagel: 1 whole egg plus 4-5 egg whites, scrambled, served on 1 bagel
2	P/O	Crispy lettuce wrap: 2-3 oz. turkey breast and cheese, rolled with large lettuce leaf	**Mocha Protein Shake** (See page 90.)
3	P/V/O	Chicken Caesar salad: 3-4 oz. chicken on large lettuce and cucumber salad, with 1 tbsp. extra-virgin olive oil and vinegar (croutons OK)	Chicken Caesar salad: 6-8 oz. chicken on large lettuce and cucumber salad, with 1 tbsp. extra-virgin olive oil and vinegar (croutons OK)
4	SA or A	1-2 slices pizza—meat OK but not extra cheese (*Don't stuff*)	2-3 slices pizza—meat OK but not extra cheese (*Don't stuff*)
5	SA	Breakfast for dinner: Pancakes and 1 sausage link (*Don't stuff*)	Breakfast for dinner: Pancakes and 1 sausage link (*Don't stuff*)
Type Key			
P = Protein S = Starch V = Vegetable O = Fat A = Fruit			
SA = Sweets and Alcohol			

Notes

1. This sample food plan is for a nondiabetic carb-up day. If, after trying this plan, you feel lethargic or sickly, you may be carb-sensitive, and the following diabetic carb-up plan may work better for you.

2. This sample food plan shows five meals. If you consume only four meals, you may skip meal 2.

3. If you're not exercising, have only one carb-up meal as the last meal of the day.

4. Wait until after day 21 to consume cakes, other sweet starches, or alcohol.

5. Don't overeat at your carb-up meal. Eat until you are satisfied, not stuffed.

6. If you would like to substitute a different food at any particular meal, you must follow the type listed next to that meal and substitute the same type of food from your substitution list.

Your Notes

_____

_____

_____

_____

_____

_____

_____

_____

Macro-Patterning Cycle Meal Planner D: Saturday, Carb-Up Day (Diabetic)

MEAL	TYPE	WOMEN	MEN
1	P/S	1 whole egg plus 2-3 egg whites, scrambled Breakfast potatoes 1 slice toast	1 whole egg plus 4-5 egg whites, scrambled Breakfast potatoes 1 slice toast
2	P/A	½ cup cottage cheese with ½ cup fruit (any kind)	**Mocha Protein Shake** (See page 90.)
3	P/SA	6-in. sub sandwich 1 small bag chips	6-in. sub sandwich 1 small bag chips
4	P/SA	Crispy lettuce wrap: 2-3 oz. turkey breast and cheese, rolled in large leaf lettuce 1 cup berries or melon	Vanilla shake with berries or banana: 30-40 g vanilla protein powder blended with 10-12 oz. water, ½ cup fruit, and ice for desired thickness
5	SA	Pasta with chicken and sauce 1 roll (*Don't stuff*)	Pasta with chicken and sauce 1 roll (*Don't stuff*)

Type Key
P = Protein   S = Starch   V = Vegetable   O = Fat   A = Fruit
SA = Sweets and Alcohol

Notes

1. This sample food plan is for a carb-up day for people with diabetes. The idea is to have small amounts of carbs through your day with protein. Individuals who are sensitive to carbs also may prefer using this plan.

2. This plan shows five meals. If you consume only four meals, you may skip meal 2.

3. Wait until after day 21 to consume any cakes, other sweet starches, or alcohol.

4. Don't overeat at carb-up meals. Eat until you are satisfied, not stuffed.

5. If you would like to substitute a different food at any particular meal, you must follow the type listed next to that meal and substitute the same type of food from your substitution list.

Your Notes

_____

_____

_____

_____

_____

_____

_____

_____

_____

Macro-Patterning Cycle Meal Planner B:
Sunday, Baseline Day

MEAL	TYPE	WOMEN	MEN
1	P/S	**Wendy's Crepe** (See page 116.)	**Wendy's Crepe** (See page 116.)
2	P/O	Crispy lettuce wrap: 2–3 oz. turkey breast and cheese rolled with large lettuce leaf	**Mocha Protein Shake** (See page 90.)
3	P/S/V	4 oz. chicken and veggie stir-fry ½ cup rice	6 oz. chicken and veggie stir-fry ½ cup rice
4	P/O	**Orange Dream Protein Shake** (See page 89.)	**Orange Dream Protein Shake** (See page 89.)
5	P/V/O	**Tasty Turkey Taco Salad** (See page 254.)	**Tasty Turkey Taco Salad** (See page 254.)
6	FF	1 serving sugar-free gelatin with 1 tbsp. Reddi-wip spray cream (not Cool Whip)	1 serving sugar-free gelatin with 1 tbsp. Reddi-wip spray cream (not Cool Whip)
Type Key			
P = Protein S = Starch V = Vegetable O = Fat FF = Free Food			

Notes

1. This sample food plan shows five meals and a sixth free-food meal. If you consume only four meals, you may skip meal 2 or 4, for a total of four meals that day.

2. Make sure to consume one starch in two different meals before 3:00 P.M.

3. If you would like to substitute a different food at any particular meal, you must follow the type listed next to that meal and substitute the same type of food from your substitution list.

Your Notes

_____

_____

_____

_____

_____

_____

_____

_____

_____

_____

_____

_____

_____

"I Never Felt Deprived"

Linda Chamberlain

Like many women, I have struggled with my weight all my life. While I was active as a child, played basketball, and competed at the national level in the sport of baton twirling, I always felt "overweight." After college and once I finished competing in my sport, I took up jogging for weight management. I began working for a top athletic sportswear company in Oregon and was encouraged to work out on our lunch hour. I started training for marathons and exercised a minimum of six days a week. Always carrying an extra ten to fifteen pounds, I starved myself to maintain my weight. I couldn't seem to really get the balance of health I was looking for.

After a few life-changing events, I finally drew a line in the sand and decided to step over it and get my physical condition in order. I followed a weight-lifting, aerobic exercise, and eating plan that gave me great success and helped me get to my best shape ever. At forty, I was in better shape than at any other time in my life. However, I had difficulty maintaining the weight I was most comfortable at.

After a year of slowly putting weight back on, I was introduced to Wendy's eight-week Nutrition Boot Camp. I learned so much about the scientific reasoning behind eating particular foods, exercising, and how our bodies respond to exercise and fuel. I couldn't believe how the weight melted off of my body, even though I never felt deprived. I loved the variety of the food throughout the week

*and that I could have a couple days a week to basi-
cally eat more of the foods I love.*

*Now, whenever I feel like my eating or weight
level is getting a little out of control, I can pull out
the eight-week plan and get right back on track.
Life stress can become an obstacle, but now I have
a comprehensive program at my fingertips.*

This program rocks!

Cycle 3: Accelerated Fat-Loss Cycle

Don't let the intimidating name fool you; the Accelerated Fat-Loss Cycle will look very familiar, because the types of each day are the same. You will still have carb-down, baseline, and carb-up days, only now the order will be a bit different.

The following samples include one full week of daily meal plans for the Accelerated Fat-Loss Cycle. Even though we are ramping up the fat-loss cycle, you will not feel deprived. That's because you still have many food choices, and the same substitution lists are available for you to change up your menus and add variety. This cycle is about overcoming your body's continuous quest to adapt and keep fat around. We won't let that happen, so stick to your plan, and be wise to review your meal choices daily.

Accelerated Fat-Loss Cycle Meal Planner C: Monday, Carb-Down Day

MEAL	TYPE	WOMEN	MEN
1	P/S	Eggs on EZ slice of toast: 1 whole egg plus 2–3 egg whites, cooked like an omelet and served on 1 slice buttered Ezekiel toast	Eggs on EZ slice of toast: 1 whole egg plus 4–5 egg whites, cooked like an omelet and served on 1 slice buttered Ezekiel toast
3	P/V	3–4 oz. grilled chicken Lettuce wraps with cabbage, cucumber, onion, tomato, and salsa	6 oz. grilled chicken Lettuce wraps with cabbage, cucumber, onion, tomato, and salsa
4	P/O	**Mocha Protein Shake** (See page 90.)	**Mocha Protein Shake** (See page 90.)
5	P/V/V	4–6 oz. **Great Grilled Shrimp Kebabs** (See page 261.) 1 cup broccoli Salad with tomato, cucumber, and 1 tbsp. extra-virgin olive oil and vinegar or low-calorie, low-sugar dressing	6–8 oz. **Great Grilled Shrimp Kebabs** (See page 261.) 1 cup broccoli Salad with tomato, cucumber, and 1 tbsp. extra-virgin olive oil and vinegar or low-calorie, low-sugar dressing
6	P	Crispy lettuce wrap: 3–4 oz. turkey breast and 1–2 slices cheese, rolled in large Bibb lettuce leaf with mustard or light mayonnaise	**Orange Dream Protein Shake** (See page 89.)
Type Key			
P = Protein S = Starch V = Vegetable O = Fat			

Notes

1. This sample food plan shows six meals. If you consume only four meals, you may skip meal 2 or 4 and meal 6, for a total of four meals that day.

2. If you consume only five meals, then you may skip meal 2 or 4 or 6, for a total of five meals.

3. If you would like to substitute a different food at any particular meal, you must follow the type listed next to that meal and substitute the same type of food from your substitution list.

4. Make sure to eat one starch in one meal before 3:00 P.M.

Your Notes

_____

_____

_____

_____

_____

_____

_____

_____

_____

_____

_____

Accelerated Fat-Loss Cycle Meal Planner C:
Tuesday, Carb-Down Day

MEAL	TYPE	WOMEN	MEN
1	P/S	Power oats: ½ cup oatmeal prepared with cinnamon and 2 packets sugar substitute; stir in 15–20 g protein powder (check label for protein gram amount)	Power oats: ¾ cup oatmeal prepared with cinnamon and 2 packets sugar substitute; stir in 20–30 g protein powder (check label for protein gram amount)
2	P/O	½ cup cottage cheese (2 percent fat)	1 cup cottage cheese (2 percent fat)
3	P/V	Tomato stuffed with 3–4 oz. tuna, dill, and diced celery Salad with cucumber and 1 tbsp. extra-virgin olive oil and vinegar	Tomato stuffed with 6–8 oz. tuna, dill, and diced celery Salad with cucumber and 1 tbsp. extra-virgin olive oil and vinegar
4	P/O	Chocolate raspberry shake: 20–25 g chocolate protein powder added to 10–12 oz. premade Crystal Light raspberry drink	Chocolate raspberry shake: 30–40 g chocolate protein powder added to 10–12 oz. premade Crystal Light raspberry drink
5	P/V/V	4 oz. filet mignon 1 cup broccoli Salad with tomato, cucumber, and 1 tbsp. extra-virgin olive oil and vinegar or low-calorie, low-sugar dressing	6–8 oz. filet mignon 1 cup broccoli Salad with tomato, cucumber, and 1 tbsp. extra-virgin olive oil and vinegar or low-calorie, low-sugar dressing
6	P	**Orange Dream Protein Shake** (See page 89.)	**Orange Dream Protein Shake** (See page 89.)

Type Key
P = Protein   S = Starch   V = Vegetable   O = Fat

Notes

1. This sample food plan shows six meals. If you consume only four meals, you may skip meal 2 or 4 and meal 6, for a total of four meals that day.

2. If you consume only five meals, then you may skip meal 2 or 4 or 6, for a total of five meals.

3. If you would like to substitute a different food at any particular meal, you must follow the type listed next to that meal and substitute the same type of food from your substitution list.

4. Make sure to eat one starch in one meal before 3:00 P.M.

Your Notes

_____

_____

_____

_____

_____

_____

_____

_____

_____

_____

_____

_____

Accelerated Fat-Loss Cycle Meal Planner D: Wednesday, Carb-Up Day (Nondiabetic)

MEAL	TYPE	WOMEN	MEN
1	P/S	Eggs on a bagel: 1 whole egg plus 2-3 egg whites, scrambled and served on ½ bagel	Eggs on a bagel: 1 whole egg plus 4-5 egg whites, scrambled and served on 1 bagel
2	P/O	½ cup cottage cheese ½ cup berries	Vanilla shake with berries or banana: 30-40 g vanilla protein powder blended with 10-12 oz. water, ½ cup fruit, and ice for desired thickness
3	P/V/O	Crispy lettuce wrap: 3-4 oz. turkey breast and 1-2 slices cheese, rolled in large Bibb lettuce leaf with mustard or light mayonnaise	Crispy lettuce wrap: 6 oz. turkey breast and 1-2 slices cheese, rolled in large Bibb lettuce leaf with mustard or light mayonnaise
4	SA or A	1-2 slices pizza—meat OK but not extra cheese (*Don't stuff*)	2-3 slices pizza—meat OK but not extra cheese (*Don't stuff*)
5	SA	Breakfast for dinner: pancakes, sausage link, and blueberry muffin (*Don't stuff*)	Breakfast for dinner: pancakes, sausage link, and blueberry muffin (*Don't stuff*)

Type Key

P = Protein   S = Starch   V = Vegetable   O = Fat   A = Fruit

SA = Sweets and Alcohol

Notes

1. This sample food plan is for a nondiabetic carb-up day. If, after trying this plan, you feel lethargic or sickly, you may be carb-sensitive, and the following diabetic carb-up plan may work better for you.

2. This sample food plan shows five meals. If you consume only four meals, you may skip meal 2.

3. If you're not exercising, have only one carb-up meal as the last meal of the day.

4. Wait until after day 21 to consume any cakes, other sweet starches, or alcohol.

5. Don't overeat at your carb-up meal. Eat until you are satisfied, not stuffed.

6. If you would like to substitute a different food at any particular meal, you must follow the type listed next to that meal and substitute the same type of food from your substitution list.

Your Notes

_____

_____

_____

_____

_____

_____

_____

_____

Accelerated Fat-Loss Cycle Meal Planner D: Wednesday, Carb-Up Day (Diabetic)

MEAL	TYPE	WOMEN	MEN
1	P/S	1 whole egg plus 2–3 egg whites, scrambled Breakfast potatoes 1 slice toast	1 whole egg plus 4–5 egg whites, scrambled Breakfast potatoes 1 slice toast
2	P/O	½ cup cottage cheese	Chocolate raspberry shake: 30–40 g chocolate protein powder added to 10–12 oz. premade Crystal Light raspberry drink
3	P/SA	6-in. sub sandwich 1 small bag chips	6-in. sub sandwich 1 small bag chips
4	P/SA	Crispy lettuce wrap: 3–4 oz. turkey breast and 1–2 slices cheese, rolled in large Bibb lettuce leaf with mustard or light mayonnaise	Crispy lettuce wrap: 6 oz. turkey breast and 1–2 slices cheese, rolled in large Bibb lettuce leaf with mustard or light mayonnaise
5	SA	Pasta with seafood and any sauce 1 roll (*Don't stuff*)	Pasta with seafood and any sauce 1 roll (*Don't stuff*)

Type Key

P = Protein   S = Starch   O = Fat   SA = Sweets and Alcohol

Notes

1. This sample food plan is for a carb-up day for people with diabetes. The idea is to have small amounts of carbs through your day with protein. Individuals who are sensitive to carbs also may prefer using this plan.

2. This plan shows five meals. If you consume only four meals, you may skip meal 2.

3. Wait until after day 21 to consume any cakes, other sweet starches, or alcohol.

4. Don't overeat at carb-up meals. Eat until you are satisfied, not stuffed.

5. If you would like to substitute a different food at any particular meal, you must follow the type listed next to that meal and substitute the same type of food from your substitution list.

Your Notes

_____

_____

_____

_____

_____

_____

_____

_____

_____

Accelerated Fat-Loss Cycle Meal Planner B:
Thursday, Baseline Day

MEAL	TYPE	WOMEN	MEN
1	P/S	**Wendy's Crepe** (See page 116.)	**Wendy's Crepe** (See page 116.)
2	P/O	**Mocha Protein Shake** (See page 90.)	**Mocha Protein Shake** (See page 90.)
3	P/S/V	3–4 oz. roasted turkey breast 1 cup green beans ½ cup garlic mashed potato	6 oz. roasted turkey breast 1 cup green beans ½ cup garlic mashed potato
4	P/O	Chocolate raspberry shake: 20–25 g chocolate protein powder added to 10–12 oz. premade Crystal Light raspberry drink	**Orange Dream Protein Shake** (See page 89.)
5	P/V/O	**Wendy's Turkey Burgers on Un-Buns** (See page 135.) Side salad	**Wendy's Turkey Burgers on Un-Buns** (See page 135.) Side salad
6	FF	1 serving sugar-free gelatin with 1 tbsp. Reddi-wip spray cream (not Cool Whip)	1 serving sugar-free gelatin with 1 tbsp. Reddi-wip spray cream (not Cool Whip)

Type Key

P = Protein   S = Starch   V = Vegetable   O = Fat   FF = Free Food

Notes

1. This sample food plan shows five meals and a sixth free-food meal. If you consume only four meals, you may skip meal 2 or 4 for a total of four meals that day.

2. Make sure to consume one starch in two different meals before 3:00 P.M.

3. If you would like to substitute a different food at any particular meal, you must follow the type listed next to that meal and substitute the same type of food from your substitution list.

Your Notes

_____

_____

_____

_____

_____

_____

_____

_____

_____

_____

_____

Accelerated Fat-Loss Cycle Meal Planner C: Friday, Carb-Down Day

MEAL	TYPE	WOMEN	MEN
1	P/O	**Mushroom and Spinach Omelet** (See page 88.)	**Mushroom and Spinach Omelet** (See page 88.)
2	P/O	½ cup cottage cheese	1 cup cottage cheese
3	P/S/V	EZ turkey and cheese sandwich: just add mustard, lettuce, and tomato Small side salad with vinaigrette dressing	EZ turkey and cheese sandwich: just add mustard, lettuce, and tomato Small side salad with vinaigrette dressing
4	P/O	**Mocha Protein Shake** (See page 90.)	**Mocha Protein Shake** (See page 90.)
5	P/V/O	4–6 oz. **Rachel's Balsamic Grilled Chicken** (See page 134.) 1 cup asparagus Salad with tomato, cucumber, and 1 tbsp. extra-virgin olive oil and vinegar or low-calorie, low-sugar dressing	8 oz. **Rachel's Balsamic Grilled Chicken** (See page 134.) 1 cup asparagus Salad with tomato, cucumber, and 1 tbsp. extra-virgin olive oil and vinegar or low-calorie, low-sugar dressing
6	P	Chocolate raspberry shake: 20–25 g chocolate protein powder added to 10–12 oz. premade Crystal Light raspberry drink	Chocolate raspberry shake: 30–40 g chocolate protein powder added to 10–12 oz. premade Crystal Light raspberry drink

Type Key
P = Protein   S = Starch   V = Vegetable   O = Fat

Notes

1. This sample food plan shows six meals. If you consume only four meals, you may skip meal 2 or 4 and meal 6, for a total of four meals that day.

2. If you consume only five meals, then you may skip meal 2 or 4 or 6, for a total of five meals.

3. If you would like to substitute a different food at any particular meal, you must follow the type listed next to that meal and substitute the same type of food from your substitution list.

4. Make sure to eat one starch in one meal before 3:00 P.M.

Your Notes

_____

_____

_____

_____

_____

_____

_____

_____

_____

_____

_____

_____

Accelerated Fat-Loss Cycle Meal Planner D: Saturday, Carb-Up Day (Nondiabetic)

MEAL	TYPE	WOMEN	MEN
1	P/S	**Southwestern Omelet** (See page 244.) ½ cup breakfast potatoes 1 slice toast	**Southwestern Omelet** (See page 244.) ½ cup breakfast potatoes 2 slices toast
2	P	Chocolate raspberry shake: 20–25 g chocolate protein powder added to 10–12 oz. premade Crystal Light raspberry drink	Chocolate raspberry shake: 30–40 g chocolate protein powder added to 10–12 oz. premade Crystal Light raspberry drink
3	P/SA	Pulled pork sandwich 1 small order french fries (*Don't stuff*)	Pulled pork sandwich 1 small order french fries (*Don't stuff*)
4	SA or A	1 package peanut butter crackers	1 package peanut butter crackers
5	P/SA	Steak fajitas Dessert (*Don't stuff*)	Steak fajitas Dessert (*Don't stuff*)

Type Key
P = Protein   S = Starch   A = Fruit   SA = Sweets and Alcohol

Notes

1. This sample food plan is for a nondiabetic carb-up day. If, after trying this plan, you feel lethargic or sickly, you may be carb-sensitive, and the following diabetic carb-up plan may work better for you.

2. This sample food plan shows five meals. If you consume only four meals, you may skip meal 2.

3. If you're not exercising, have only one carb-up meal as your last meal of the day.

4. Wait until after day 21 to consume any cakes, other sweet starches, or alcohol.

5. Don't overeat at your carb-up meal. Eat until you are satisfied, not stuffed.

6. If you would like to substitute a different food at any particular meal, you must follow the type listed next to that meal and substitute the same type of food from your substitution list.

Your Notes

_____

_____

_____

_____

_____

_____

_____

_____

_____

Accelerated Fat-Loss Cycle Meal Planner D:
Saturday, Carb-Up Day (Diabetic)

MEAL	TYPE	WOMEN	MEN
1	P/S	1 whole egg plus 2–3 egg whites, scrambled ½ cup breakfast potatoes 1 slice toast	1 whole egg plus 4–5 egg whites, scrambled ½ cup breakfast potatoes 1 slice toast
2	P	Chocolate raspberry shake: 20–25 g chocolate protein powder added to 10–12 oz. premade Crystal Light raspberry drink	Chocolate raspberry shake: 30–40 g chocolate protein powder added to 10–12 oz. premade Crystal Light raspberry drink
3	P/SA	Pulled pork sandwich 1 small order french fries (*Don't stuff*)	Pulled pork sandwich 1 small order french fries (*Don't stuff*)
4	SA	1 package peanut butter crackers	1 package peanut butter crackers
5	P/SA	Steak fajitas Dessert (*Don't stuff*)	Steak fajitas Dessert (*Don't stuff*)

Type Key

P = Protein   S = Starch   SA = Sweets and Alcohol

Notes

1. This sample food plan is for a carb-up day for people with diabetes. The idea is to have small amounts of carbs through your day with protein. Individuals who are sensitive to carbs also may prefer using this plan.

2. This plan shows five meals. If you consume only four meals, you may skip meal 2.

3. Wait until after day 21 to consume any cakes, other sweet starches, or alcohol.

4. Don't overeat at carb-up meals. Eat until you are satisfied, not stuffed.

5. If you would like to substitute a different food at any particular meal, you must follow the type listed next to that meal and substitute the same type of food from your substitution list.

Your Notes

_____

_____

_____

_____

_____

_____

_____

_____

_____

_____

Accelerated Fat-Loss Cycle Meal Planner B: Sunday, Baseline Day

MEAL	TYPE	WOMEN	MEN
1	P/S	**Wendy's Bull's-Eye Breakfast** (See page 133.)	**Wendy's Bull's-Eye Breakfast** (See page 133.)
2	P	**Orange Dream Protein Shake** (See page 89.)	**Orange Dream Protein Shake** (See page 89.)
3	P/S/V	Chinese lunch: 4 oz. chicken and veggie stir-fry on ½ cup rice	Chinese lunch: 6 oz. chicken and veggie stir-fry on ½ cup rice
4	P/O	½ cup cottage cheese	1 cup cottage cheese
5	P/V/O	4 oz. filet mignon 1 cup asparagus Salad with tomato, cucumber, and 1 tbsp. extra-virgin olive oil and vinegar or low-calorie, low-sugar dressing	6–8 oz. filet mignon 1 cup asparagus Salad with tomato, cucumber, and 1 tbsp. extra-virgin olive oil and vinegar or low-calorie, low-sugar dressing
6	FF	1 serving sugar-free gelatin with 1 tbsp. Reddi-wip spray cream (not Cool Whip)	1 serving sugar-free gelatin with 1 tbsp. Reddi-wip spray cream (not Cool Whip)

Type Key
P = Protein   S = Starch   V = Vegetable   O = Fat   FF = Free Food

Notes

1. This sample food plan shows five meals and a sixth free-food meal. If you consume only four meals, you may skip meal 2 or 4, for a total of four meals that day.

2. Make sure to consume one starch in two different meals before 3:00 P.M.

3. If you would like to substitute a different food at any particular meal, you must follow the type listed next to that meal and substitute the same type of food from your substitution list.

Your Notes

_____

_____

_____

_____

_____

_____

_____

_____

_____

_____

_____

_____

_____

Cycle 4: Maintenance Cycle

We've compared the body to a car so often in this book that I thought it would be good to do it once more. Just as you maintain a car in between breakdowns—with oil changes and tune-ups and tire pressure gauges—the body needs some maintenance, too.

The Maintenance Cycle is a must, especially if you still want to lose weight once you have learned to crack the fat-loss code. It is important to implement this cycle to restore hormone and chemical levels in the body that actually aid in fat loss.

The Maintenance Cycle, or some variation of it, can also be used indefinitely once you have reached your fat-loss goals. If you wish to lose more weight after your initial eight weeks, you should follow the Maintenance Cycle for at least two weeks before you start your macro-patterning plan again.

Code Cracker

Information without action isn't any way to crack the fat-loss code, so now it's time to use all that information and put it into action.

Notice that during this new cycle, you add two other types of days: your cheat day (CH), or Food Pass, and a high-carb day (H). Also notice that there is a new type of baseline day, called maintenance baseline, which, for those who enjoy it, allows you to consume fruit every day. (Remember, on this food plan, it is not recommended that people with diabetes consume fruit at all.) Following is a complete week's worth of sample daily meal plans to get you started.

"Let's All Chant for Wendy!"

Jacob D. Rouse, M.D.

Wendy Chant, what an incredible lady! Her energy and enthusiasm are contagious, and her ForeverFit lifestyle program is truly a blessing. My patients, friends, and colleagues have all lost weight. I have just begun her plan and find it very easy to follow, and I feel great. Don't say can't; let's all chant for Wendy!

Code Cracker

Don't let appearance rule your life. Fat loss is just one aspect of who you are.

Maintenance Cycle Meal Planner B:
Monday, Baseline Day

MEAL	TYPE	WOMEN	MEN
1	P/S or A	**Wendy's Crepe** (See page 116.)	**Wendy's Crepe** (See page 116.)
2	P or A	1 apple	1 cup of fruit
3	P/S/V	3–4 oz. roasted turkey breast 1 cup green beans ½ cup garlic mashed potato	6 oz. roasted turkey breast 1 cup green beans ½ cup garlic mashed potato
4	P/O	**Mocha Protein Shake** (See page 90.)	**Mocha Protein Shake** (See page 90.)
5	P/V/O	4–6 oz. **Great Grilled Shrimp Kebabs** (See page 261.) 1 cup broccoli Salad with tomato, cucumber, and 1 tbsp. extra-virgin olive oil and vinegar or low-calorie, low-sugar dressing	6–8 oz. **Great Grilled Shrimp Kebabs** (See page 261.) 1 cup broccoli Salad with tomato, cucumber, and 1 tbsp. extra-virgin olive oil and vinegar or low-calorie, low-sugar dressing
6	FF	1 serving sugar-free gelatin with 1 tbsp. Reddi-wip spray cream (not Cool Whip)	1 serving sugar-free gelatin with 1 tbsp. Reddi-wip spray cream (not Cool Whip)

Type Key
P = Protein   S = Starch   V = Vegetable   O = Fat   A = Fruit
FF = Free Food

Notes

1. This sample food plan shows five meals and a sixth free-food meal. If you consume only four meals, you may skip meal 2 or 4. If you skip meal 2, you may have your fruit in place of a starch in meal 1.

2. At meal 1 have a protein with a starch or fruit, not both. If you have a starch at meal 1, then you may have a fruit without a protein at meal 2. If you have a fruit with your protein at meal 1, then have just a protein at meal 2.

3. If you would like to substitute a different food at any particular meal, you must follow the type listed next to that meal and substitute the same type of food from your substitution list.

Your Notes

_____

_____

_____

_____

_____

_____

_____

_____

_____

_____

_____

Maintenance Cycle Meal Planner B:
Tuesday, Baseline Day

MEAL	TYPE	WOMEN	MEN
1	P/S or A	**Power Oats** (See page 117.)	**Power Oats** (See page 117.)
2	P or A	1 cup berries (any kind)	Vanilla shake with berries or banana: 30–40 g vanilla protein powder blended with 10–12 oz. water, ½ cup fruit, and ice for desired thickness
3	P/S/V	3–4 oz. grilled chicken in wrap Salad with tomato, cucumber, and 1 tbsp. extra-virgin olive oil and vinegar or low-calorie, low-sugar dressing	6 oz. grilled chicken in wrap Salad with tomato, cucumber, and 1 tbsp. extra-virgin olive oil and vinegar or low-calorie, low-sugar dressing
4	P	**Mocha Protein Shake** (See page 90.)	**Mocha Protein Shake** (See page 90.)
5	P/V/O	4–6 oz. **Rachel's Balsamic Grilled Chicken** (See page 134.) 1 cup asparagus Salad with tomato, cucumber, and 1 tbsp. extra-virgin olive oil and vinegar or low-calorie, low-sugar dressing	8 oz. **Rachel's Balsamic Grilled Chicken** (See page 134.) 1 cup asparagus Salad with tomato, cucumber, 1 tbsp. extra-virgin olive oil and vinegar or low-calorie, low-sugar dressing
6	FF	1 serving sugar-free gelatin with 1 tbsp. Reddi-wip spray cream (not Cool Whip)	1 serving sugar-free gelatin with 1 tbsp. Reddi-wip spray cream (not Cool Whip)

Type Key
P = Protein   S = Starch   V = Vegetable   O = Fat   A = Fruit
FF = Free Food

Notes

1. This sample food plan shows five meals and a sixth free-food meal. If you consume only four meals, you may skip meal 2 or 4. If you skip meal 2, you may have your fruit in place of a starch at meal 1.

2. At meal 1, have a protein with a starch or fruit, not both. If you have a starch at meal 1, then you may have a fruit without a protein at meal 2. If you have a fruit with your protein at meal 1, then have just a protein at meal 2.

3. If you would like to substitute a different food at any particular meal, you must follow the type listed next to that meal and substitute the same type of food from your substitution list.

Your Notes

_____

_____

_____

_____

_____

_____

_____

_____

_____

_____

_____

Maintenance Cycle Meal Planner B:
Wednesday, Baseline Day

MEAL	TYPE	WOMEN	MEN
1	P/S or A	Vanilla shake with berries or banana: 25 g vanilla protein powder blended with 10 oz. water, ½ cup fruit, and ice for desired thickness	Vanilla shake with berries or banana: 30–40 g vanilla protein powder blended with 10–12 oz. water, ½ cup fruit, and ice for desired thickness
2	P or A	½ cup cottage cheese (2 percent fat)	1 cup cottage cheese (2 percent fat)
3	P/S/V	**Wendy's Turkey Burgers on Un-Buns** (See page 135.) Side salad ½ baked potato with ½ tsp. butter	**Wendy's Turkey Burgers on Un-Buns** (See page 135.) Side salad ½ baked potato with ½ tsp. butter
4	P/O	**Orange Dream Shake** (See page 89.)	**Orange Dream Shake** (See page 89.)
5	P/V/O	4–6 oz. **Great Grilled Shrimp Kebabs** (See page 261.) 1 cup broccoli Salad with tomato, cucumber, and 1 tbsp. extra-virgin olive oil and vinegar or low-calorie, low-sugar dressing	6–8 oz. **Great Grilled Shrimp Kebabs** (See page 261.) 1 cup broccoli Salad with tomato, cucumber, 1 tbsp. extra-virgin olive oil and vinegar or low-calorie, low-sugar dressing
6	FF	1 serving sugar-free gelatin with 1 tbsp. Reddi-wip spray cream (not Cool Whip)	1 serving sugar-free gelatin with 1 tbsp. Reddi-wip spray cream (not Cool Whip)

Type Key
P = Protein   S = Starch   V = Vegetable   O = Fat   A = Fruit
FF = Free Food

Notes

1. This sample food plan shows five meals and a sixth free-food meal. If you consume only four meals, you may skip meal 2 or 4. If you skip meal 2, you may have your fruit in place of a starch in meal 1.

2. At meal 1, have a protein with a starch or fruit, not both. If you have a starch at meal 1, then you may have a fruit without a protein at meal 2. If you have a fruit with your protein at meal 1, then have just a protein at meal 2.

3. If you would like to substitute a different food at any particular meal, you must follow the type listed next to that meal and substitute the same type of food from your substitution list.

Your Notes

_____

_____

_____

_____

_____

_____

_____

_____

_____

_____

_____

Maintenance Cycle Meal Planner B:
Thursday, Baseline Day

MEAL	TYPE	WOMEN	MEN
1	P/S or A	**Wendy's Crepe** (See page 116.)	**Wendy's Crepe** (See page 116.)
2	P or A	1 apple	1 cup of fruit, any kind
3	P/S/V	3–4 oz. roasted turkey breast 1 cup green beans ½ cup garlic mashed potato	6 oz. roasted turkey breast 1 cup green beans ½ cup garlic mashed potato
4	P/O	**Mocha Protein Shake** (See page 90.)	**Mocha Protein Shake** (See page 90.)
5	P/V/O	4–6 oz. broiled salmon or halibut 1 cup steamed asparagus Salad with tomato, cucumber, and 1 tbsp. extra-virgin olive oil and vinegar or low-calorie, low-sugar dressing	8 oz. broiled salmon or halibut 1 cup steamed asparagus Salad with tomato, cucumber, and 1 tbsp. extra-virgin olive oil and vinegar or low-calorie, low-sugar dressing
6	FF	1 serving sugar-free gelatin with 1 tbsp. Reddi-wip spray cream (not Cool Whip)	1 serving sugar-free gelatin with 1 tbsp. Reddi-wip spray cream (not Cool Whip)

Type Key
P = Protein   S = Starch   V = Vegetable   O = Fat   A = Fruit
FF = Free Food

Notes

1. This sample food plan shows five meals and a sixth free-food meal. If you consume only four meals, you may skip meal 2 or 4. If you skip meal 2, you may have your fruit in place of a starch at meal 1.

2. At meal 1, have a protein with a starch or fruit, not both. If you have a starch at meal 1, then you may have a fruit without a protein at meal 2. If you have a fruit with your protein at meal 1, then have just a protein at meal 2.

3. If you would like to substitute a different food at any particular meal, you must follow the type listed next to that meal and substitute the same type of food from your substitution list.

Your Notes

_____

_____

_____

_____

_____

_____

_____

_____

_____

_____

_____

Maintenance Cycle Meal Planner B:
Friday, Baseline Day

MEAL	TYPE	WOMEN	MEN
1	P/S or A	**Wendy's Bull's-Eye Breakfast** (See page 133.)	**Wendy's Bull's-Eye Breakfast** (See page 133.)
2	P or A	½ cup cottage cheese with ½ cup berries	1 cup fruit, any kind
3	P/S/V	3–4 oz. top sirloin steak with mushrooms 1 cup broccoli ½ baked potato with ½ tsp. butter	6–8 oz. top sirloin steak with mushrooms 1 cup broccoli ½ baked potato with ½ tsp. butter
4	P/O	Chocolate raspberry shake: 20–25 g chocolate protein powder added to 10–12 oz. premade Crystal Light raspberry drink	Chocolate raspberry shake: 30–40 g chocolate protein powder added to 10–12 oz. premade Crystal Light raspberry drink
5	P/V/O	4–6 oz. grilled chicken 1 cup green beans with garlic Salad with tomato, cucumber, and 1 tbsp. extra-virgin olive oil and vinegar or low-calorie, low-sugar dressing	6–8 oz. grilled chicken 1 cup green beans with garlic Salad with tomato, cucumber, and 1 tbsp. extra-virgin olive oil and vinegar or low-calorie, low-sugar dressing
6	FF	1 serving sugar-free gelatin with 1 tbsp. Reddi-wip spray cream (not Cool Whip)	1 serving sugar-free gelatin with 1 tbsp. Reddi-wip spray cream (not Cool Whip)

Type Key
P = Protein   S = Starch   V = Vegetable   O = Fat   A = Fruit
FF = Free Food

Notes

1. This sample food plan shows five meals and a sixth free-food meal. If you consume only four meals, you may skip meal 2 or 4. If you skip meal 2, you may have your fruit in place of a starch at meal 1.

2. At meal 1, have a protein with a starch or fruit, not both. If you have a starch at meal 1, then you may have a fruit without a protein at meal 2. If you have a fruit with your protein at meal 1, then have just a protein at meal 2.

3. If you would like to substitute a different food at any particular meal, you must follow the type listed next to that meal and substitute the same type of food from your substitution list.

Your Notes

_____

_____

_____

_____

_____

_____

_____

_____

_____

_____

_____

_____

Maintenance Cycle Meal Planner CH: Saturday, Cheat Day

MEAL	TYPE	WOMEN	MEN
1	S	½ bagel with cream cheese	1 bagel with cream cheese
2	S	**Mocha Protein Shake** (See page 90.)	**Mocha Protein Shake** (See page 90.)
3	S	½ 6-in. sub sandwich 1 snack bag chips	1 6-in. sub sandwich 1 snack bag chips
4	S	Pizza or pasta dinner Dessert	Pizza or pasta dinner Dessert
5	S/A	**Orange Dream Protein Shake** (See page 89.)	**Orange Dream Protein Shake** (See page 89.)

Type Key
P = Protein   S = Starch   V = Vegetable   O = Fat   A = Fruit
FF = Free Food

Notes

1. Eat whatever you want in any amount.

2. Timing isn't necessary on cheat day.

3. Follow this meal plan if you're afraid you might go overboard.

4. Relax! It is a free day, well deserved.

5. Be careful with sweets and alcohol. You may have them on this day, but don't overconsume.

Your Notes

_____

_____

_____

_____

_____

_____

_____

_____

_____

_____

_____

_____

_____

_____

_____

_____

Maintenance Cycle Meal Planner H:
Sunday, High-Carb Day

MEAL	TYPE	WOMEN	MEN
1	P/S or A	**Power Oats** (See page 117.)	**Power Oats** (See page 117.)
2	P or A	1 apple	1 cup of fruit, any kind
3	P/S/V	3–4 oz. roasted turkey breast 1 cup green beans ½ sweet potato	6 oz. roasted turkey breast 1 cup green beans 1 sweet potato
4	P/O	Chocolate raspberry shake: 20–25 g chocolate protein powder added to 10–12 oz. premade Crystal Light raspberry drink	Chocolate raspberry shake: 30–40 g chocolate protein powder added to 10–12 oz. premade Crystal Light raspberry drink
5	P/S/V	4 oz. filet mignon ½ baked potato Salad with tomato, cucumber, 1 tbsp. extra-virgin olive oil and vinegar or low-calorie, low-sugar dressing	6–8 oz. filet mignon 1 baked potato Salad with tomato, cucumber, 1 tbsp. extra-virgin olive oil and vinegar or low-calorie, low-sugar dressing
6	FF	1 serving sugar-free gelatin with 1 tbsp. Reddi-wip spray cream (not Cool Whip)	1 serving sugar-free gelatin with 1 tbsp. Reddi-wip spray cream (not Cool Whip)

Type Key

P = Protein   S = Starch   V = Vegetable   O = Fat   A = Fruit

FF = Free Food

Notes

1. This sample food plan shows five meals and a sixth free-food meal. If you consume only four meals, you may skip meal 2 or 4. If you skip meal 2, you may have your fruit in place of a starch at meal 1.

2. At meal 1, have a protein with a starch or fruit, not both. If you have a starch at meal 1, then you may have a fruit without a protein at meal 2. If you have a fruit with your protein at meal 1, then have just a protein at meal 2.

3. If you would like to substitute a different food at any particular meal, you must follow the type listed next to that meal and substitute the same type of food from your substitution list.

Your Notes

_____

_____

_____

_____

_____

_____

_____

_____

_____

_____

_____

11

Charting Your Success

Sample Log Sheets

I have always found that, when it comes to health at least, very little can be left to chance. Planning is the foundation on which fat is lost and stays off, so I encourage you to keep a log book. The pages that follow are log sheets for you to keep track of your daily food intake. There is a specific sheet for each cycle day on your plan. Also included on the logs is a reminder key of what macronutrient combination to have at each meal. The beauty of these log sheets is that you can duplicate them at home or your nearest copy shop and simply fill them in.

Please don't think this is an "extra" or "optional" step just because it's found near the back of your book. These log sheets were specifically designed to be used every day, no matter what cycle or day you're on in the cycle, so use them!

Logging your foods is a very important part of your success. Not only does it give you a guide to follow, but continuing to log your daily consumption is a great means of accountability as well.

Carb-Deplete Day (A) Food Log

Week Day: _____ Week Date: _____ Rising Time: _____ Bedtime: _____

MEAL	TIME	TYPE	FOOD ITEM
1		P/O	
2		P/O	
3		P/V/O	
4		P/O	
5		P/V/O	
6		P/O	

Type Key
P = Protein   V = Vegetable   O = Fat

Baseline Day (B) Food Log

Week Day: _____ Week Date: _____ Rising Time: _____ Bedtime: _____

MEAL	TIME	TYPE	FOOD ITEM
1		P/S	
2		P/O	
3		P/S/V	
4		P/O	
5		P/V/V	
6		P/O	

Type Key
P = Protein   V = Vegetable   O = Fat   S = Starch

Carb-Down Day (C) Food Log

Week Day: _____ Week Date: _____ Rising Time: _____ Bedtime: _____

MEAL	TIME	TYPE	FOOD ITEM
1		P/S	
2		P	
3		P/V/V	
4		P	
5		P/V/V	
6		P/O	

Type Key
P = Protein   V = Vegetable   O = Fat   S = Starch

Carb-Up Day (D) Food Log

Week Day: _____ Week Date: _____ Rising Time: _____ Bedtime: _____

MEAL	TIME	TYPE	FOOD ITEM
1		P/S	
2		P/O	
3		SA or A	
4		P/O	
5		SA or A	
6		P	

Type Key
P = Protein   O = Fat   S = Starch   A = Fruit SA = Sweets and Alcohol

12

ForeverFit Eating

More of Wendy's
"Mmm Good" Recipes

The beauty of the food plan in *Crack the Fat-Loss Code* is that—get this—there are *no forbidden foods* after the Carb-Deplete Cycle, so feel free to try any of your favorite recipes. In addition to my favorite recipes included in each cycle section, this section offers some of the favorites given to us by other "code crackers." Just make sure you check the ingredients and follow your day's cycle plan for complete success.

Breakfast Favorites

Bodybuilder's Rice Pudding

Use planners B, C, D

> ¼ cup Cream of Rice
>
> 1 scoop vanilla American Whey or other lower-carb
>   protein powder
>
> 1 packet sugar substitute

Prepare Cream of Rice per box instructions, adding a little more water to make a runny consistency. Pour into bowl, and add protein powder. Mix thoroughly, and add sugar substitute. Nutritional value based on using American Whey.

1 serving

Nutritional Value
Protein: 20 grams
Fat: trace
Carbs: 44 grams

Power Pancakes

Use planners B and D

> 2 eggs
>
> 4 tablespoons ricotta cheese (or cream cheese)
>
> Dash cinnamon and nutmeg
>
> 2 packets sugar substitute (optional)
>
> Nonstick cooking spray

Mix together eggs, cheese, cinnamon, nutmeg, and sugar substitute. Spray nonstick cooking spray on to skillet, and pour batter in, spreading a little. Brown on one side; flip, and brown on other side. This tastes great, especially with maple syrup. If it's difficult to flip, cut the pancake in half.

1 big serving

Nutritional Value
Protein: 18 grams
Fat: 17 grams
Carbs: 4 grams

Anytime Egg Favorites

Southwestern Omelet

Use planners A, B, C, D

> 4 medium fresh mushrooms, sliced
>
> 1 whole egg plus 3 egg whites (for women), or 2 whole eggs plus 5 egg whites (for men), or use egg substitute
>
> ¼ cup fresh or frozen spinach (if frozen, thaw and press out excess moisture)
>
> 2 tablespoons salsa
>
> ¼ cup cottage cheese
>
> ⅛ cup shredded cheddar (or your favorite) cheese

Spray skillet with nonstick cooking spray; place over medium heat. Add mushrooms, and cook 1 to 2 minutes. Beat eggs and egg whites; pour over mushrooms, and move mushrooms to one side of pan. Layer spinach, salsa, and cottage cheese over mushrooms. When eggs are cooked to desired doneness, fold the egg-only side over the other half; sprinkle with cheese.

1 serving

Nutritional Value
Protein: 22 grams / 41 grams
Fat: 4 grams / 6 grams
Carbs: 6.5 grams

Cheesy Mushroom Omelet

Use planners A, B, C, D

   4 medium fresh mushrooms, sliced

   1 whole egg plus 3 whites (for women), or 2 whole
      eggs plus 5 egg whites (for men), or use egg
      substitute

   ¼ cup grated cheddar cheese

Spray skillet with nonstick cooking spray; place over medium heat. Add mushrooms, and cook 1 to 2 minutes. Beat eggs and egg whites; pour over mushrooms and cook until set. Fold over, and top with cheese. Serve with sliced tomatoes if desired. (Remember to add nutritional values for tomatoes if used.)

1 serving

Nutritional Value
Protein: 16 grams / 29 grams
Fat: 4 grams / 6 grams
Carbs: 3 grams

Quiche

Use planners B and D

> 2 to 4 slices of Ezekiel bread, enough to cover bottom
> of pan
>
> 9 eggs or equivalent combination of egg whites and whole eggs
>
> 1 8-ounce block cheddar-flavored tofu
>
> Parmesan cheese

Preheat oven to 350°F. Spray a 13″ × 9″ pan with olive oil cooking spray. Line pan with bread. Beat eggs. Crumble tofu in food processor. Mix with eggs. Pour mixture over bread, and sprinkle with Parmesan cheese. Bake 1 hour.

4 servings

Nutritional Value
Protein: 20 grams
Fat: 5 grams
Carbs: 4 grams

Mushroom, Broccoli, and Egg Muffins

Use planners B and D

> Nonstick cooking spray
>
> 1 pound mushrooms, thinly sliced
>
> 1 large head broccoli, cut into florets
>
> 1½ teaspoons olive oil
>
> 6 ounces cheddar cheese, shredded (or substitute
> any cheese you like)
>
> Salt and pepper to taste
>
> 6 whole eggs plus 6 egg whites

Preheat oven to 350°F. Spray muffin tins with nonstick spray; set aside. Spray large skillet with nonstick spray. Add mushrooms, and sauté until browned and crusty on the edges, 10 to 15 minutes.

While mushrooms are cooking, steam broccoli until tender. Place broccoli in a mixing bowl; add olive oil, and mash lightly with a fork until chunky. Add the mushrooms. Cool to room temperature. Mix in cheese, salt, and pepper. Fill each muffin tin ¾ full with the mushroom-broccoli mixture. Beat eggs in a bowl with a splash of water until light and fluffy; season with salt and pepper. Pour the eggs over the vegetables in muffin tins. Bake approximately 10 to 15 minutes (eggs will be set on top). Serve immediately, or wrap each muffin and store in refrigerator or freezer.

6 muffins

Nutritional Value
Protein: 9.5 grams
Fat: 5 grams
Carbs: 5 grams

Egg Crepes

Use planners A, B, C, D

> 3 whole eggs plus 3 egg whites
>
> Salt and pepper to taste
>
> Nonstick cooking spray

In a mixing bowl, lightly beat eggs and egg whites. Season with salt and pepper. Heat a crepe or omelet pan over medium-high heat, and coat bottom with nonstick cooking spray. Ladle into the pan enough egg to make a thin coating. When it sets, lift up with a spatula, being careful not to tear the crepe, and turn. Cook 1 more minute, and then slide the crepe out of the pan onto a dish. Continue until all batter is used. Stack crepes as you would pancakes.

1 serving

Nutritional Value
Protein: 28 grams
Fat: 6 grams
Carbs: 0 grams

Salad and Side Dish Favorites

Donielle's Summer Salad

Use planners B and D

> 2 cups chopped broccoli florets
>
> 2 cups chopped cauliflower florets
>
> 1 small red bell pepper
>
> 1 medium cucumber
>
> ½ cup chopped red onion
>
> 1 16-ounce container reduced-fat sour cream
>
> 1 packet original Hidden Valley Ranch dip mix

Chop broccoli, cauliflower, pepper, cucumber, and onion into bite-size pieces. Mix the sour cream with the dip mix, and then add to the vegetable mixture. Chill for at least 1 hour before serving. (You may substitute any combination of your favorite vegetables.)

12 ½-cup servings

Nutritional Value
Protein: 3 grams
Fat: 4 grams
Carbs: 5 grams

Diane's Unfried French Fries

Use planners B and D

> 5 large baking potatoes
>
> 2 egg whites
>
> 1 tablespoon Cajun spice

Move oven rack to bottom level, and preheat oven to 400°F. Slice each potato lengthwise into ¼-inch ovals, and then slice each oval into matchsticks. Coat a baking sheet with 3 sprays of nonstick cooking spray. Combine the egg whites and Cajun spice in a bowl. Add the matchstick potatoes, and mix to coat. Pour the coated potatoes on the prepared baking sheet, and spread into a single layer, leaving a little space around each piece. Bake on bottom oven rack for 40 to 45 minutes, until fries are crispy, turning every 6 to 8 minutes.

5 servings

Nutritional Value
Protein: trace
Fat: 0 grams
Carbs: 44 grams

Zucchini Chips

Use planners B, C, D

2 large zucchini

1 tablespoon extra-virgin olive oil

¼ teaspoon salt

¼ teaspoon garlic powder (optional)

Preheat oven to 400°F. Coat 2 baking sheets with nonstick cooking spray. Thinly slice zucchinis ⅛ inch thick. Place slices in a large bowl, and toss well with olive oil, salt, and garlic powder. Arrange in a single layer on baking sheets. Bake, turning often, 25 minutes. Reduce temperature to 300°F, and bake until splotchy brown and crisp, 10 to 15 minutes. Remove and place in a single layer on paper towels, and let cool. These will keep at room temperature uncovered for several hours.

4 servings

Nutritional Value
Protein: 2 grams
Fat: 3 grams
Carbs: 5 grams

Cucumber Salad

Use planners B, C, D

> 4 cucumbers
>
> 2 tablespoons salt (for "pickling")
>
> 2 tablespoons sour cream
>
> 2 tablespoons fresh dill
>
> 1 clove garlic, minced
>
> Chopped chives or green onions
>
> Salt and pepper to taste

Peel cucumbers, quarter lengthwise, and scrape out seeds; slice at an angle into little disks. Add salt, mix well, and set aside for 1 hour or more. (The longer they sit, the more "pickled" the cucumber pieces will be.) Rinse thoroughly and press out extra liquid with a paper towel (as much as you can without smashing cucumbers). Rinse and press out extra liquid again. Taste; if too salty, repeat the rinsing process. Stir in sour cream, dill, and garlic; add chives or green onions, salt, and pepper to taste. Chill at least 1 hour. Stir again and serve.

1 serving

Nutritional Value
Protein: trace
Fat: 5 grams
Carbs: 2 grams

Spicy Thai Chicken Salad

Use planners B, C, D

Salad

> 2 cups chopped cooked chicken breast
>
> 2 cups red bell pepper strips
>
> 1 cup sliced celery
>
> 1 cup thinly sliced red onion
>
> 1 cup sliced cucumber
>
> ½ cup coarsely chopped cilantro
>
> 1 7-ounce package Italian blend salad greens

Dressing

> 3 tablespoons fresh lemon juice
>
> 2 tablespoons fish sauce
>
> 1 tablespoon sesame seeds, toasted
>
> 1 teaspoon sugar substitute
>
> 1 teaspoon ground ginger
>
> ½ teaspoon crushed red pepper

Combine chicken, bell pepper, celery, onion, cucumber, cilantro, and salad greens in a bowl. To prepare dressing, whisk together lemon juice, fish sauce, sesame seeds, sugar substitute, ginger, and red pepper. Drizzle dressing over salad, and toss well.

5 servings (3 cups)

Nutritional Value
Protein: 19 grams
Fat: 3.5 grams
Carbs: 12 grams

Tasty Turkey Taco Salad

1 tablespoon olive oil

¼ onion, chopped

½ pound lean ground turkey

¼ teaspoon oregano

¾ teaspoon chili powder

¼ teaspoon black pepper

½ teaspoon salt

1 small can stewed tomatoes, drained

1 packet sugar substitute

1 ounce cheddar cheese, grated

Romaine lettuce

Heat the oil in a skillet. Add onion and sauté until soft. Add turkey and brown until meat is cooked through. Drain fat and add seasonings. Mix well. Add tomatoes and sugar substitute; stir to combine. Bring to a boil, reduce heat, cover, and simmer for 10 minutes. Uncover and cook an additional 5 minutes. Add cheese, stirring until melted. Serve over lettuce.

2 servings

Nutritional Value
Protein: 27 grams
Fat: 10 grams
Carbs: 4 grams

Skillet Broccoli Rice

Use planners B, C, D

    2 cups chopped fresh broccoli florets

    1 10¾-ounce can condensed 98 percent fat-free
        broccoli-cheese soup

    1⅓ cups reduced-sodium chicken broth

    Pepper to taste

    2 cups instant rice, uncooked

Arrange broccoli in a steamer basket over boiling water. Cover and steam 3 to 4 minutes or until broccoli is just crisp. Combine soup, broth, and pepper in a large nonstick skillet, stirring with a whisk until smooth. Bring to a boil. Stir in rice and broccoli. Cover, reduce heat, and simmer 5 to 6 minutes or until liquid is absorbed and rice is tender. Fluff with a fork before serving.

8 servings

Nutritional Value
Protein: 3 grams
Fat: 1 grams
Carbs: 19 grams

Oriental Green Beans

Use planners B, C, D

> 1½ pounds fresh green beans
>
> 1 tablespoon sesame or olive oil
>
> 3 tablespoons soy sauce
>
> 1 tablespoon sugar substitute
>
> 6 garlic cloves, minced

Cook green beans to desired doneness. Mix together oil, soy sauce, sugar substitute, and garlic. Drain green beans well, and toss with sauce.

1 serving

Nutritional Value
Protein: trace
Fat: 14 grams
Carbs: 3 grams

Chicken and Fish Favorites

Stuffed Peppers with Chicken and Broccoli

Use planners B and D

> 1 cup broccoli
>
> 1 3.5-ounce can pure white cooked chicken (or cooked fresh chicken, cut into small pieces)
>
> 1 tablespoon mayonnaise
>
> 2 red bell peppers
>
> ⅛ cup of your favorite cheese, shredded

Cook broccoli until tender, and let cool. You may want to stick broccoli in the fridge, depending on how cold you want it to be. Mix chicken and mayonnaise, and add the chilled broccoli. Leave in fridge until at desired temperature. Cut the peppers in half, and clean out all seeds. Spoon chicken mixture into pepper shells, and sprinkle a little cheese on top.

Note: This is also good on a carb-up day. Instead of bell peppers, serve the chicken salad on a croissant.

1 serving

Nutritional Value
Protein: 30 grams
Fat: 3 grams
Carbs: 10 grams

Chicken Oreganata

Use planners B and D

> 1 cup fresh lemon juice (juice of about 5 lemons)
>
> 2 tablespoons extra-virgin olive oil
>
> 1½ tablespoons minced garlic
>
> 1½ teaspoons dried oregano
>
> 2 pounds boneless, skinless chicken thighs (about 8)
>
> ¼ teaspoon salt
>
> 1 teaspoon black pepper

Combine lemon juice, olive oil, garlic, and oregano in a zip-top plastic bag; add chicken. Seal and refrigerate 3 hours or overnight, turning occasionally.

Preheat oven to 350°F. Remove chicken from bag; discard marinade. Place chicken in a single layer on a broiler pan coated with nonstick cooking spray. Sprinkle with salt and pepper. Bake 30 minutes or until chicken is done.

Note: You may substitute breasts for the thighs, but nutritional values will change.

4 servings (2 thighs per serving)

Nutritional Value
Protein: 45 grams
Fat: 16 grams
Carbs: 8 grams

Crispy Chicken Lettuce Wraps

3 tablespoons olive oil

2 medium boneless, skinless chicken breasts, cut
    into pieces or use 1 pack of chicken tenders

1 teaspoon fresh grated gingerroot

2 teaspoons rice vinegar

2 teaspoons teriyaki sauce

1 or 2 packets of sugar substitute

½ cup mushrooms, chopped

½ cup water chestnuts, chopped

2 tablespoons chopped green onions

4 lettuce leaves

Heat large skillet over medium-high heat and add oil. Add
chicken and ginger and sauté until cooked through (about 7
minutes). Set aside. Whisk together the remaining 1 tablespoon
oil, vinegar, teriyaki sauce, and sugar substitute. When cool
enough to handle, chop chicken; return to skillet along with
sauce, mushrooms, water chestnuts, and green onions. Cook for
a few minutes to warm and combine. Divide mixture among lettuce leaves and roll to make wraps.

2 servings

Nutritional Value
Protein: 27 grams
Fat: 3 grams
Carbs: 6 grams

Tuna Pancake

Use planners B, C, D

> 1 6-ounce can low-sodium tuna
>
> ⅓ cup Coach's Oats or regular oatmeal
>
> 1 egg and 2 egg whites or 3 egg whites

Mix all ingredients thoroughly. Coat skillet with canola oil, or spray with nonstick cooking spray. Sauté tuna mixture on both sides.

1 serving

Nutritional Value
Protein: 24 grams
Fat: 2 grams
Carbs: 12 grams

Great Grilled Shrimp Kebabs

1 pound shrimp, peeled and deveined (thawed if
      frozen)

½ bottle Italian dressing

1 red bell pepper, cut into 1″ pieces

1 pound cremini or whole button mushrooms

Place shrimp in plastic sealable bag and add half of Italian
dressing. Place pepper and mushrooms in another bag and add
remaining dressing. Marinate in refrigerator for at least 2 hours.
Discard marinade and thread on metal or soaked wooden skewers. Grill kebabs until shrimp is cooked through, about 3 minutes each side.

4 servings

Nutritional Value
Protein: 21 grams
Fat: 4 grams
Carbs: 6 grams

Grilled Tilapia Fillet

Use planners B, C, D

> 1 4- or 5-ounce tilapia fillet
>
> ½ onion, thinly sliced
>
> Adobo Criollo seasoning (available in the Hispanic
> section of many grocery stores)

Use a skillet or table-top grill, such as the George Foreman grill. Season tilapia and onion with Adobo Criollo seasoning. Coat skillet with nonstick cooking spray or a small amount of olive oil or prepare grill. Sauté or grill fillet until done. Then sauté or grill onion until golden brown.

The trick to this recipe is the seasoning. Make sure to season the onion, too.

1 serving

Nutritional Value
Protein: 28 grams
Fat: 2 grams
Carbs: 2 grams

Appendix A

Body Fat Calculator

Let's face it: when all is said and done, this is a book about losing fat. Notice I didn't say "losing pounds" or "losing weight." I said losing fat. But how do you know if you've lost fat if you don't know how much was there to begin with?

There are many ways to calculate body fat. Some are more accurate than others. Most fitness centers will measure your body fat if you are a member, but the key is to have the same person calculating each time to ensure accuracy.

For your convenience—and to be able to perform this check yourself—Dr. Fred Hatfield, known as Dr. Squat, devised a quick calculator that you can use to get an idea of what your body fat measures before, during, and after you have gotten used to the macro-patterning cycles of *Crack the Fat-Loss Code.*

Of course, you can always use my closet method, which is pretty darn simple: Walk into your closet, look way in the back where you have that favorite pair of jeans that you haven't fit into for years, and try them on. If they are getting easier to pull on and zip up, well, you know your body fat is going down!

But if you'd like something just a bit more "scientific," here is a surefire method:

Your Body Fat Estimator

1. Multiply your weight: _____ × 1.082 = _____
   (weight nude)   (nude factor)

2. Add nude factor: _____ + 94.42 = _____
   (nude factor)   (weight factor)

3. Take waist measurement: _____ × 4.150 = _____
   (at navel)   (waist factor)

4. _____ − _____ = _____
   (weight factor)   (waist factor)   (lean body mass)

5. _____ − _____ = _____
   (weight nude)   (lean body mass)   (your body fat)

6. _____ ÷ _____ × 100 = _____
   (your body fat)   (weight nude)   (your % body fat)

Appendix B

Metric Conversion Chart

Volume Measurement Conversions

U.S.	Metric
¼ teaspoon	1.25 ml
½ teaspoon	2.5 ml
¾ teaspoon	3.75 ml
1 teaspoon	5 ml
1 tablespoon	15 ml
¼ cup	62.5 ml
½ cup	125 ml
¾ cup	187.5 ml
1 cup	250 ml

Weight Conversion Measurements

U.S.	Metric
1 ounce	28.4 g
8 ounces	227.5 g
16 ounces (1 pound)	455 g

Cooking Temperature Conversions

On the Celsius and centigrade scales, 0°C and 100°C are arbitrarily placed at the melting and boiling points of water and standard to the metric system.

Fahrenheit established 0°F as the stabilized temperature when equal amounts of ice, water, and salt are mixed.

To convert temperatures in Fahrenheit to Celsius, use this formula:

$$C = (F - 32) \times 0.5555$$

So, for example, if you are baking at 350°F and want to know that temperature in Celsius, use this calculation:

$$C = (350 - 32) \times 0.5555 = 176.65°C$$

References and Scientific Basis

This section provides sources of supportive data and an explanation of the major scientific points of *Crack the Fat-Loss Code*.

Seventy-Two-Hour Reserve Function

All supportive data is the same time-tested data already used in the "gold standard" diet books, which include the Atkins, South Beach, and *Body for Life* diets. This scientific point is based on carbohydrate depletion and the biochemistry of glycogen. In short, it takes three days (seventy-two hours) in an average mildly active individual to deplete the skeletal muscle of carbohydrates (glycogen). This section offers a brief explanation of glycogen biochemistry and a partial listing of relevant studies. Literally hundreds of studies have been used, for purposes of marathon runners, extreme sport racers, and bodybuilders. Dieters benefit from these studies for fat loss as well.

Biochemistry of Glycogen

Glycogen is found principally in muscle and liver cells, where it serves as a readily accessible depot for the storage of glucose. Glycogen is broken down when adenosine triphosphate (ATP) transfers intracellular energy needed by muscle cells or when blood glucose levels drop too low over a seventy-two-hour period. Glycogen is composed of linked D-glucose residues.

FIGURE R.1   Glucose Linkage Residue

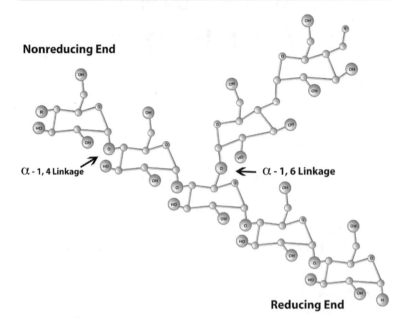

Nonreducing End

α - 1, 4 Linkage

← α - 1, 6 Linkage

Reducing End

The linkages between glucose residues are of two types: α-1,4 and α-1,6, shown in Figure R.1. The importance of glycogen to our plan is in the understanding of the importance of how glycogen converts to energy. The energy is what we manipulate to ultimately satisfy the body's needs of replenishing glycogen and using fat as a source of energy, thus the creation of macro-patterning.

Sources

Alonso M. D., J. Lomako, W. M. Lomako, and W. J. Whelan. 1995. "A New Look at the Biogenesis of Glycogen." *Federation of American Societies for Experimental Biology Journal* 9(12): 1126–37.

Baba, N. H., S. Sawaya, N. Torbay, A. Habbal, S. Azar, and S. A. Hashim. 1999. "High Protein vs. High Carbohydrate Hypoenergetic Diet for the Treatment of Obese

Hyperinsulinemic Subjects." *International Journal of Obesity and Related Metabolic Disorders* 23(11): 1202–6.

Bergström, J., L. Hermansen, E. Hultman, and B. Saltin. 1967. "Diet, Muscle Glycogen and Physical Performance." *Acta Physiologica Scandinavica* 71(2): 140–50.

Biolo, G., R. Y. Declan Fleming, and R. R. Wolfe. 1995. "Physiologic Hyperinsulinemia Stimulates Protein Synthesis and Enhances Transport of Selected Amino Acids in Human Skeletal Muscle." *Journal of Clinical Investigation* 95(2): 811–19.

Burke, L. M., G. R. Collier, and M. Hargreaves. 1993. "Muscle Glycogen Storage After Prolonged Exercise: Effect of the Glycemic Index of Carbohydrate Feedings." *Journal of Applied Physiology* 75(2): 1019–23.

Costill, D. L., W. M. Sherman, and W. J. Fink. 1981. "The Role of Dietary Carbohydrate in Muscle Glycogen Resynthesis after Strenuous Running." *American Journal of Clinical Nutrition* 34: 1831–36.

Coyle, E. F. 1991. "Timing and Method of Increased Carbohydrate Intake to Cope with Heavy Training, Competition and Recovery." *Journal of Sports Science and Medicine* 9 (suppl): 29–52.

Danforth W. H. 1965. "Glycogen Synthetase Activity in Skeletal Muscle: Interconversion of Two Forms and Control of Glycogen Synthesis." *Journal of Biological Chemistry* 240 (February): 588–93.

Hers, H. G., and L. Hue. 1983. Gluconeogenesis and Related Aspects of Glycolysis." *Annual Review of Biochemistry* 52: 617–53.

Ivy, J. L., M. C. Lee, and M. J. Reed. 1988. "Muscle Glycogen Storage After Different Amounts of Carbohydrate Ingestion." *Journal of Applied Physiology* 65:20,018–23.

Kirsch, K. A., and H. von Ameln. 1981. "Feeding Patterns of Endurance Athletes." *European Journal of Applied Physiology* 47: 197–208.

Roberts, K. M., E. G. Noble, D. B. Hayden, and A. W. Taylor. 1988. "Simple and Complex Carbohydrate-Rich Diets and Muscle Glycogen Content of Marathon Runners." *European Journal of Applied Physiology* 57: 70–74.

Forty-Eight-Hour Conserve Function

The body's conservation of energy expenditure is well supported by many medical and scientific studies done on how restrictive food intake or harsh dieting affects the metabolic rate. Energy expenditure encompasses many factors, including resting metabolic rate (RMR), thermic effect of food (TEF), thermic effect of activity (TEA), and thermic effect of stress (TES). All these factors play a role in the total energy expenditure. Along with the following partial list of relevant studies, there are hundreds of studies that date from 1969 to the present day.

Sources

Abbott, W., et al. 1990. "Energy Expenditure in Humans: Effects of Dietary Fat and Carbohydrate." *American Journal of Physiology* 258 (2 pt. 1): E347–E351.

Booth, Frank, Ph.D. "University of Missouri at Columbia study concluded that the fat cells in lab rats can increase in size by 25% after 48 hours of missed exercise." *Women's Health*, March 2007.

Borel, M., et al. 1984. "Estimation of Energy Expenditure and Maintenance Energy Requirements of College-Age Men and Women." *American Journal of Clinical Nutrition* 40(6): 1264–72.

Bray, G. 1969. "Effect of Caloric Intake on Energy Expenditure in Obese Subjects." *Lancet* 2: 397–98.

Brillon, D., et al. 1995. "Effect of Cortisol on Energy Expenditure and Amino Acid Metabolism in Humans." *American Journal of Physiology* 268: E501–E513.

Bullough, C. R., C. A. Gilette, M. A. Harris, and C. L. Melby. 1995. "Interaction of Acute Changes in Exercise Energy

Expenditure and Energy Intake on Resting Metabolic Rate." *American Journal of Clinical Nutrition* 61: 473–81.

deGroot, L., et al. 1989. "Adaptation of Energy Metabolism of Overweight Women to Alternating and Continuous Low Energy Intake." *American Journal of Clinical Nutrition* 50(6): 1314–23.

Foster, G., et al. 1990. "Controlled Trial of the Metabolic Effects of a Very-Low-Calorie Diet: Short- and Long-Term Effects." *American Journal of Clinical Nutrition* 51(2): 167–72.

Garby, L., et al. 1988. "Effect of 12 Weeks' Light-Moderate Underfeeding on 24-Hour Energy Expenditure in Normal Male and Female Subjects." *European Journal of Clinical Nutrition* 42(4): 295–300.

Henson, L., et al. 1987. "Effects of Exercise Training on Resting Energy Expenditure During Caloric Restriction." *American Journal of Clinical Nutrition* 46(6): 893–99.

Lee, R., and D. Nieman. 2003. *Nutritional Assessment*, 3rd ed. Boston: McGraw-Hill, 233.

Luscombe, N., et al. 2002. "Effects of Energy-Restricted Diets Containing Increased Protein on Weight Loss, Resting Energy Expenditure and Thermic Effect of Feeding in Type II Diabetes." *Diabetes Care* 25(4): 652–57.

Molé, P. A., J. S. Stern, C. L. Schultz, E. M. Bernauer, and B. J. Holcomb. 1989. "Exercise Reverses Depressed Metabolic Rate Produced by Severe Caloric Restriction." *Medicine and Science in Sports and Exercise* 21(1): 29–33.

Mulligan, K., and G. E. Butterfield. 1990. "Discrepancies Between Energy Intake and Expenditure in Physically Active Women." *British Journal of Nutrition* 64: 23–36.

Utter, A. C., D. C. Nieman, E. M. Shannonhouse, D. E. Butterworth, and C. N. Nieman. 1998. "Influence of Diet and/or Exercise on Body Composition and Cardiorespiratory Fitness in Obese Women." *International Journal of Sport Nutrition* 8(3): 213–22.

Velthuis-te Weirik, E., et al. 1995. "Impact of a Moderately Energy Restricted Diet on Energy Metabolism and Body Composition in Non-Obese Men." *International Journal of Obesity and Related Metabolic Disorders* 19(5): 318–24.

Adaptive Response—Dieter's Plateau

The regulating by the body of its intake and expenditure is the major key to understanding the set-point theory of body weight. It is said that the hypothalamus and autonomic nervous system achieve something known by the body as homeostasis, or maintaining the body's status quo. Factors such as blood pressure, body temperature, fluid and electrolyte balance, and body weight are held to a precise value called the set point. Although this set point can migrate over time, from day to day it is remarkably fixed. To be successful over the long term, any diet must overcome the body's response to adapt. The set-point theory is a very old scientific study that has resurfaced recently and has made its way into many recent diet books. The following articles are just a small selection of the cited research on the set-point theory.

Sources

Chant, W. L. 2003. "The Body's Adaptive Ability Explained." Altamonte Springs, FL: *ForeverFit Nutrition Boot Camp Advanced Manual.*

Harris, R. B. 1990. "Role of Set-Point Theory in Regulation of Body Weight." *Federation of American Societies for Experimental Biology Journal* 4: 3310–18.

Keesey, R. E., and M. D. Hirvonen. 1997. "Body Weight Set-Points: Determination and Adjustment." *Journal of Nutrition* 127 (suppl.): 1875S–1883S.

More About ForeverFit Programs and Services

Now that we've gotten to know each other a little better, I'd like to introduce you to the full line of ForeverFit programs and services offered at our national headquarters in Central Florida as well as online at joinforeverfit.com. Take a look through the following categories, and see which program and/or service best fits your needs.

When you're ready, simply click, write, or call, and I'll be glad to personally help you crack the fat-loss code on a whole new level. Enjoy!

- **Crack the Fat-Loss Code with Nutrition Boot Camp DVD:** For your convenience, the entire eight-week program using the *Crack the Fat-Loss Code* philosophy is available on a one-of-a-kind DVD uniquely designed to walk you through the program week by week. Through this entertaining and informative DVD, you can educate yourself on all the vital information about your body and how it responds to food. You will also hear the stories of countless boot camp "code crackers" who have changed their lives forever using this revolutionary program. The DVD comes with a companion guide that has the entire eight-week daily menu with easy substitutions list and also a recipe booklet and log book for you to keep track of your progress. Visit our website at www.joinforeverfit.com to watch a preview and to see Rachel's story of her dramatic 165-pound weight loss using the *Crack the Fat-Loss Code* program.

• **Eight-week classes in Central Florida and national weekend boot camps:** *Crack the Fat-Loss Code* began as an informative class format for people seeking the truth about fat loss and dieting. Since then, these one-of-a-kind programs have been attended by thousands, and Wendy Chant, today's fitness authority, not only guides her students to fat-loss success, but also gives information and advice on exercise, supplementation, and how to achieve a better body. Remember our motto: "Better health and better life."

• **Exclusive food coaching with Wendy Chant—in person, online, and by phone and fax:** Couldn't everyone use a food coach? Well, you can't go wrong when Wendy Chant personally guides you through the *Crack the Fat-Loss Code* process. She takes a personal interest in all her students' success. Whether you're right in front of her or thousands of miles away, you will never have guilt or worries about food when Wendy is your coach.

• **Website resources and member area:** The ForeverFit website is incredibly resourceful, with such features as an events calendar, forums, and a section where you can ask questions, look for advice, or share your stories with others. Also included on the site, free of charge, are exercise and workout plans and video downloads. Just added is a huge recipe database that will give you appetizing solutions for your meal planning. The online store even has the ForeverFit supplement line, personally developed with Wendy's stringent quality specifications. The store has all the top-quality protein powders suggested by Wendy.

• **Toll-free number:** You can always reach ForeverFit on our toll-free number at (866) 865-9110 or contact us through our website, joinforeverfit.com. Or if you're visiting Florida, why not stop by our corporate offices in Altamonte Springs?

Index

About the Author

Wendy Chant's impressive credentials surpass the already rigorous standards required in the competitive and demanding field of nutrition sciences. She is a certified Master Personal Trainer (MPT) and Specialist in Performance Nutrition (SPN), with a bachelor of science degree in medical sciences and nutrition science. Maybe that's why she is known nationally as "Today's Fitness Authority."

Beginning her career as a personal trainer with Bally Total Fitness, Wendy quickly achieved a national ranking as one of the top ten in personal training. Her commitment to helping others achieve their goals inspired the opening of her own training studio, ForeverFit, in 1998.

As a Specialist in Performance Nutrition, Wendy was one of the first in her field to truly embrace the philosophy of food coaching. Food coaching is tailored to a client's particular goals, with the aim of making that person feel fantastic on all levels: health, vitality, moods, and weight, as well as confident in his or her food choices and body image. By analyzing her clients' diets and providing them with education and alternatives, she has since become a sought-after food coach, not just locally but nationally. In fact, her coaching has been so successful that Wendy has her own line of supplements to help clients take matters into their own hands.

A former marathon runner and champion bodybuilder who competed on the national level, Wendy has since focused all of her attention on spreading the ForeverFit message. From her corporate offices in Central Florida, she divides her busy schedule between running her individual Nutrition Boot Camp classes and nurturing a full speaking schedule, holding seminars and workshops for the likes of FedEx, AT&T, and Disney.